CREATION

CREATION

David Pawson

ANCHOR

Copyright ©2024 David Pawson Ministry CIO

The right of David Pawson to be identified as author of this Work has been asserted by him in accordance with the Copyright, Designs and Patents Act 1988.

First published in Great Britain in 2024 by
Anchor which is a trading name of
David Pawson Publishing Ltd,
Synegis House, 21 Crockhamwell Road,
Woodley, Reading RG5 3LE

No part of this publication may be reproduced or transmitted in any form or by any means, electronic or mechanical, including photocopy, recording or any information storage and retrieval system, without prior permission in writing from the publisher.

**For more of David Pawson's teaching,
including DVDs and CDs, go to
www.davidpawson.com**

**FOR FREE DOWNLOADS
www.davidpawson.org**

**For further information,
email: info@davidpawsonministry.org**

ISBN 978-1-913472-73-3

Printed by Ingram Spark

Contents

FOREWARD   7

CHAPTER 1: IN THE BEGINNING   9
CHAPTER 2: THE SEVEN DAYS OF CREATION   41
CHAPTER 3: THE ORIGIN OF MAN   77
CHAPTER 4: SATAN EXPOSED   115
CHAPTER 5: EVOLUTION AND ITS EFFECTS   151

This book is based on a series of talks. Originating as it does from the spoken word, its style will be found by many readers to be somewhat different from my usual written style. It is hoped that this will not detract from the substance of the biblical teaching found here. As always, I ask the reader to compare everything I say or write with what is written in the Bible and, if at any point a conflict is found, always to rely upon the clear teaching of scripture.

David Pawson

Foreword

In this book, which is drawn from a series of talks given in the early 1980s, David Pawson guides the reader from the origins of the universe, and specifically the creation of planet Earth and the human race, to the Fall and its ongoing consequences for contemporary society. He addresses the issue of Satanically inspired opposition that has sought to undermine the biblical account of Creation. In doing so, he tackles the evolution versus creation debate, an area that has long been marked by controversy and heated argument, with an approach that is both measured and nuanced, as befits such a complex subject. Characteristically, David strives to do justice to the main viewpoints before presenting his own position. Crucially, he argues that science and the book of Genesis are complementary and that much unnecessary confusion and doubt has arisen from the misapplication of Scripture. By identifying common ground, he appeals to both Scripture and modern scientific theories and findings. However, he parts company with those who claim that the universe was not created. As he notes, "once you cut out the Creator you cut out creation. Once you cut out the Originator you cut out origin. Cut God out, and there cannot be a beginning."

David discusses a number of Charles Darwin's formative experiences and critiques certain interpretations of elements of his theory of evolution. The final chapter touches on the impact of Darwin's work (and that of his followers) on belief in the traditional Christian interpretation of the account of creation in Genesis. David also explores some of the implications of these viewpoints, including their contribution to the rise of a more secular and atheistic culture. Balancing such criticism with an argument for the compatibility of a scientific perspective with Christian faith in God as Creator, David cautions against the misuse of the biblical text, pointing out that "the Bible does not

CREATION

try and argue the existence of God", but instead simply states, "In the beginning, God...". A Christian will always begin from this starting point of faith and David argues that if the believer holds to this fundamental belief, then everything else will make sense. However, he cautions that it is not the job of the Christian or the Bible to "explain God" and the problem is not God's existence but rather "the existence of this world" and "the existence of me and my sin".

Justin Byron-Davies

CHAPTER 1:

IN THE BEGINNING

We are going to study creation from Genesis chapter one to chapter three. The present chapter is very much an introduction to the other studies. I am only going to take one verse now. That will be just about all we can cope with because it is the biggest statement in the Bible. It is simply the first verse of Genesis chapter one. I shall quote it first from the Bible and then I will provide a paraphrased version of that verse. Genesis 1 verse 1 simply says this: "In the beginning, God created the heavens and the earth." And here is the paraphrased version: "A long time ago when nothing else existed, the God who had always been there brought into being the entire universe, everything in outer space and planet Earth." That is trying to express that verse in the language of today and fill it out with meaning.

The early chapters of Genesis have been for many people a source of arguments rather than answers. And some of the questions you get asked when you venture into these chapters are intriguing. "Who made God?" is one. "Was it six days or four billion years, as the scientists tell us?" One I came across recently, which was new to me, was: "Did Adam have a navel?" And that raises all sorts of questions. And "Where did Cain get his wife?" I am sure you have heard about the ape sitting in his cage in the zoo, scratching his head, and thinking "Am I my keeper's brother?" That raises the whole question of evolution versus creation.

But Genesis 1 was given to us to give us answers, not to start arguments. It is a tragedy that it has become such a controversial battlefield. Endless conflict has arisen out of these chapters. So much so that many Christians say, "Oh, well let's stick to the nice passages of the Bible on which everybody agrees. Why don't you teach us Psalm 23? That would comfort us much more and everybody agrees on how nice that is." But I want to tell you that I believe that in studying these chapters we are engaging in a battle, a warfare that is crucial. If the first sentence of the Bible is a lie, then the whole of the rest of the Bible is a lie. For the whole Bible hangs on the first sentence, and if that is not true then you cannot rely on anything else it says. It is the basic presupposition on which everything else God says is built. Let that go and you have lost the lot – that is why it is such a fierce controversy.

Why, then, go way back to the very beginning of our universe? How is that going to help me in 2023 to face unemployment, recession, inflation, nuclear disarmament? What possible connection could there be between the very beginning of our universe and where I am now? What is the relevance of studying this? Well, I would just give you two things to introduce. Number one: the past is always the key to the present. What you were will determine what you are. That is why if you apply for a job, they will ask you for a reference. They will want to know where you are coming from and what you were like there, and then they will know what you are likely to be like here.

In fact, there are a lot of things in life that you will just not understand unless you go back to the beginning. I remember being shown around the House of Commons by the then speaker, Mr George Thomas, and there are a lot of things in the House of Commons that you don't understand; in fact, crazy things. You look in the House of Commons and you see they are all sitting on two sides of the chamber. Why on earth can't they sit around in a semi-circle like most other parliaments do, instead of this "them and us" business in which they face each other like two opposing armies? No wonder they get into opposition when they are sitting like that.

Chapter 1: In the beginning

And you think, "Why do they sit like that?" The answer is that the House of Commons first met in the choir stalls of the church and that was how it began. That is why they do it now. There are two red stripes on the carpet of the floor. And you say, "What are those for?" And they say, "Well that is so that the members on this side and the members on that side can't put a foot over that red line, because that keeps them more than two swords apart." You think, "Well why on earth have that? There's not a sword in sight." But, of course, it began when members of parliament went armed to debates and you had to keep them that far apart.

You see, time and again we are asked about things that are parliamentary procedure now and we have found that you would not understand it unless you went back to the beginning. It is the same with our world. That is where we find our identity. Who am I? I had a man ring me up at three o'clock in the morning. He was drunk. He always used to ring up after he got drunk. It seemed as if he would not talk until he had got a bit of Dutch courage and he rang me up at three in the morning and he said, "Pastor, who am I?" That is quite a question to try and answer a drunk man at three in the morning.

But that is the basic question, "Who am I?" You don't understand who you are until you go back to your origins. That is why Alex Haley when he wrote the book *Roots* captured the imagination. He was a black man living in America and he didn't understand himself. He thought, "Why do I feel like I do? Who am I? Where do I fit into the scheme of things here?" So, he traced his ancestry back through that name that his great-grandmother remembered, Kunta Kinte, and he got back to Africa and found the village from which his great-great-great-grandfather had come as a slave. And he discovered who he was and he found his identity. Therefore, I want to know, did I come out of a zoo? Did I come out of a jungle? Who am I? And you can't answer that until you go right back to the beginning. So, the first reason for going right back to the beginning of all things is that the past is

CREATION

the key to the present. You will not understand the present year unless you go right back to the beginning.

The second thing is that the past is also a key to the future, because where you come from usually indicates where you are going to. "Dust thou art, and to dust thou shalt return," in other words, that is where you came from and that is where you will finish up. Where you started you will probably finish. And the world where it began will also end. If it began without God it will end without God. If it began with God it will end with God. And so, an awful lot hangs on this; the present and the future are both tied right back to the beginning. If you don't have the beginning right, you will probably misinterpret the present and the future, and get those wrong also. That covers most of my life – the past, present, and the future. I can't think of any other part of my life. So, it is vital that I get back to the beginning.

Incidentally, the end and the beginning are so closely related that if you read the first three pages of the Bible and the last three pages you'll be astonished; they are about the same things. And there are some things that disappear after the first three pages and don't come back again until the last three, things like the tree of life. It is because the beginning and the end are the same, and the complete cycle is there in the Scripture.

Now the basic question we are going to ask is, how come? When a little baby becomes self-conscious, and then conscious of the people around it, and then the places around it, sooner or later that baby will ask, "How come these people got here?" And then will ask, "How come the world got here?" It is not long before a child asks a parent, "Where did I come from?" The parent thinks, "Now is the time for the lecture. Well, the birds and the bees," and explains it all. And the little child looks puzzled and the parent asks, "Why did you ask?" "Well, the boy next door said he came from Bristol." The parent realises – they wasted an awful lot of biological explanation. But actually, what that little child is asking is, "Who am I? How did I get here? I

Chapter 1: In the beginning

know I'm here but how did I get here?" And they are asking the same basic question, how come?

What is going on is nothing less than a battle for the mind, and the people who believe the first sentence in the Bible are in a very small minority in the modern world. There are many other answers to the question, how come? We are being bombarded with them through the mass media. In every schoolroom in this land, in magazines, and in the press, this battle for the mind is going. There is a battle going on for the mind. Why should such a battle be so important? The answer is, the mind is the key to the man and if you can capture a man's mind you have got him. "As a man thinks in his heart so is he." The kind of thing you are constantly thinking about will determine the kind of person you are. Your thoughts will actually make you the character you become. What you are constantly thinking about will be you. And therefore, the battle for the mind is the battle for the man.

The Bible also tells us that we are not to be chameleons but caterpillars. You want to know where that comes? It is in Romans chapter twelve verse two. It says, "Don't be a chameleon, but be a caterpillar." Now it may not be quite like that in your versions so let me explain. What is a chameleon? If you put a chameleon on a blue carpet, it turns blue. If you put it on that red duster it will turn red. If you want to kill a chameleon you put it on tartan, and it bursts.

But Romans 12 says this: "Don't be conformed to the world around you." Don't let your mind be filled with the bombardment of other views that you are constantly getting. Don't be a chameleon. Don't agree with the latest TV programme you are seeing. It is terribly easy to pick up the thoughts outside us and let that become our thinking. That is what the chameleon does.

The caterpillar goes through a process of metamorphosis and it changes from the inside, and out of it comes a beautiful butterfly, and those have come from the inside. So Paul says, "Don't let your mind be conformed to the world around you, to the thinking

CREATION

outside you, but let it be transformed" – literally metamorphosis – "let it change from the inside." That is really what we are going to try and do in these chapters. It is so easy to pick up the world's thinking and not to let our minds be independent inside. The battle for the mind is the battle for the man.

Now I want to go further in introduction and say that I want you to realise that the battles of Genesis are not the war. There is a war being fought over Genesis 1–3 which is different from the battles. There are certain specific battles about the six days, about evolution, about where Cain got his wife. But those are only battles, they are not the war. And if you do not realise the war you might get the battles wrong. In the Falkland Islands there were battles for Bluff Cove, San Carlos, Goose Green, Stanley; but the war was with Argentina. You can get so bogged down in the battles over Genesis that you miss the war. Now, in this chapter I am not going to deal with any of the battles. I will deal with some of those in the next chapter; questions like evolution, and how long did it take, and the rest. Those are battles. In this chapter I want to deal with the war, because Genesis 1:1 is a declaration of war on every other understanding of the world in which we live.

Now to help you to understand what I am getting at I want to tell you the parable of the invisible snooker champion, because I think this will help you to understand. I got home late one night and relaxed for fifteen minutes watching the snooker championships. Fascinating.

But I want you to imagine the parable of the invisible snooker champion. It is a bit silly but try and imagine a snooker championship in which there is an invisible champion with an invisible cue. But he is playing with visible balls on a visible table. I want you to stretch your imagination further and imagine that there are two people who have been told to commentate on the championship. But one has been told, "You must only speak about the visible part of the match, the balls on the table," and

Chapter 1: In the beginning

the other is told, "Now you comment on the invisible part, on the player and how he plays." So, the two commentators commentate on this champion.

One says, "He is now going to hit the red; yes, there it goes." The other commentator takes over and says, "The red ball is travelling at a great speed down the centre of the table. It glances off the white ball; it glances off the red ball. Yes, it's not going right in the pocket." Back to the first commentator and he describes what the man will do next. He says, "Now he's going to go for the black and yes, yes he's going for the black." The second commentator takes over again and says, "Yes, the white ball is heading straight for the black. The black has hit the cushion, but it's in."

Now what am I getting at? Both these commentators are talking about the same situation and they should not normally disagree because one is talking about one part of that situation the other about the other. One is speaking of things that can't be seen, the other of things that can be seen, but they are describing the same event. If you listen to both of them you will get the total picture of what is happening. But there are two situations in which those two commentators could disagree and have an argument. The first would be the simple situation in which they disagreed about a fact.

One of them says, "He is now going to knock in the brown ball," and the other commentator says, "The blue ball has gone into the pocket." And the first man says, "I said the brown ball he was going for." "But the blue ball went in." "But it was the brown ball he was going for," and an argument strikes up. It is not a serious one because it can be easily settled by looking in the pocket. The evidence of what is the truth is available to both commentators, and they simply need to look at the evidence a bit more carefully and find out which of them was mistaken.

Was the man commenting on the ball a bit colour blind and got the colour wrong? Or was the man commentating on the player misreading the player's mind? But one or even both were mistaken, and a simple look at the evidence would tell you which one was wrong. One would be wrong in observation and the other in interpretation. But they need not have disagreed. That is a battle over fact. And the facts can simply be established, and that will settle it.

But now I want you to imagine that the game is over. The black has gone down for the last time and the two commentators have finished their work. They turn to each other and one says, "Good game," and the other says, "Very good game." And then one says, "He really played well," and the other says, "Who played well?" "Well, the player." "But there was no player." "Of course there was." "But there wasn't; I couldn't see any."

"Well how do you think those balls went down those holes?" "Well, I guess the table tipped or something in the balls made them move, but they were moving by themselves." "Now that's just plain stupid. How do you know they were moving by themselves?" "Well, I don't. But how do you know there was a player there? You can't see him." And so the argument builds up until finally it is just "There was," "There wasn't," "There was," "There wasn't," and there's a real major battle going on. But in fact, they have moved from a conflict about facts to a conflict about faith. And one is saying, "I believe there was a player playing the balls," and the other is saying "I believe there wasn't." But there is no evidence available to either to prove their case, and so they argue.

Now I hope you are following this little picture with me because I am going to say something very important. And you wonder why they are both so hot about this argument as to whether there is a player or there isn't. In fact, the man who believes there is says, "But look, those balls went down in an order. You saw them: red, black, red, black and then when just the colours were there you saw them: yellow, green, blue. There was an order and the result was the game was won. Surely you

Chapter 1: In the beginning

believe there was somebody doing all that."

"Ah well, we don't understand all the patterns and all the chance statistics," and they're awfully het up about it. You find yourself saying, "I wonder why they're getting so het up about this argument." And then you find out that the one who believes there was a player there believes he is going to get paid for his commentary afterwards. You find out that the other one who does not want to believe there is a player there has got his eye on the table and the balls, and he wants to take them home with him. Now I think you may understand where I am heading.

The whole business between science and Scripture is in that little parable. Both are looking at the same event, the beginning of the world. Science is looking at the visible part of what is happening. It is looking at the table and the balls, it is looking at the trees, it is looking at the clouds, it is looking at the stars, it is looking at every part of the event that can be seen, and it is describing how they interact, how they affect each other; whereas Scripture is looking at the part that cannot be seen. Whereas science should be saying how and when certain things happen, and what happens, Scripture will be telling you who and why, which is a different commentary.

You would expect, therefore, that Scripture and science would always agree, but that is not the case. They are both describing the same thing, and the same God we believe made the world and his Word, and therefore they ought to agree because God is a God of truth. Then why should science and Scripture ever disagree? Why should there be so much controversy about Genesis? Well, I want to tell you that the battles are battles of fact, but the warfare is a warfare of faith. And if you are with me so far you will come with me the rest of the way.

There are battles over facts. Science seems to say that this earth is four billion years old or more. Whereas Genesis seems to say it was less than a week until human history began. It does not seem to tie up. It is a difference of fact because they both

CREATION

can't be right. And whenever you come up against that difference both sides have to ask, "Did I make a mistake?" One side has to ask, "Did I make a mistake of observation?" And the other has to say, "Did I make a mistake of interpretation?" One side has to ask, "Did science really prove that?" And the other has to ask, "Did Scripture really say that?" Ultimately, those sorts of battles will be resolved by the evidence that is available to both, the evidence of stark fact. But it is the warfare that is going on that is the serious thing.

The warfare starts when the scientist says, "There is no one playing the game. This world brought itself into being. The game is being played by the game itself." And it is at that point that the war is on, and it is a very serious war.

One poem expresses the real issue. The poem goes like this: "'There is no God,' the speaker cries. 'Don't let your thoughts be chained. This universe evolved itself, the world is self contained.' Just then an urchin in the crowd a skillful pebble throws which accurately lands upon his atheistic nose. 'Who threw that stone?' the speaker roars, at which the cockney elf, intuitively keen, retorts, 'No one! It threw itself.' So, a pathetic casualty, discomfited and worse, goes home to meditate upon this causeless universe."

That is the warfare. The warfare is this, if I can sum it up. Did something produce someone or did someone produce something? That is what the war is about, and there are no middle positions in that warfare. Either we believe that something – matter, energy, or whatever you like –was always there and produced someone, and the personality was produced by things. Or we believe that someone was there, always there, who produced something. I am putting it as simply as I can. The Bible is right on one side of that warfare and every other view of man that I have come across is on the other side. That is the war. And behind all the arguments about the six days and about evolution, I want you to realise that that is what we are fighting: the view that something

Chapter 1: In the beginning

produced someone, whereas the first verse in the Bible says that someone produced something. I don't think I can put it more simply than that.

Can I take an illustration from elsewhere in the Bible to make clear what I am saying by way of introduction? Take the parting of the Red Sea, for example. Imagine it. It says in the Bible that God sent an east wind which parted the Red Sea. Now there is the sort of billiard game or snooker game I have been describing. An invisible player hits the wind, which then hits the sea, and the invisible moves the visible.

Supposing a scientist were watching all that happen, he would say, "It's easy, I can explain everything. When you saw the Red Sea part it was due to the east wind. I've explained it." And you say, "Well, it was a very happy event that it happened just when the Israelites were trapped on one side of it, wasn't it?" And he says, "Coincidence." He says, "All I can see is the natural process of the wind pushing the water, and that's all there is to it." But Scripture says the invisible, eternal God pushed the wind, which pushed the water and he saved a whole people from slavery.

Now do you see the difference? There need be no argument. If the scientist says, "Well, I'm just talking about the visible things," and the Scripture says, "We're talking about the invisible things." That is okay. Why don't we leave each other alone? Why argue farther? Now, you could have an argument about fact. The scientist might say, "Well, it was a west wind, not an east wind." And you could settle that by checking up. But the warfare would be the scientist saying, "God wasn't in that at all. It was entirely a self-contained natural process that happened by itself."

Therefore, one will talk of providence and the other will talk of coincidence. One will talk of choice and the other will talk of chance. One will live by faith and the other will live by fate. One will say, "I'm full of hope," and the other will say, "Well, I'm full of despair because I never know what my luck will be tomorrow." And if there is one thing that is riddling our society

CREATION

it is a belief in luck, right? Even at our wedding we had relatives who rushed up with a lucky horseshoe and we had to put it out of the way. We did not want that thing in our wedding photographs. We did not get married with the best of luck. We got married within providence, not coincidence. We did not get married in a universe we believed was based on chance, but on choice. We do not believe it was chance that we met; we believe it was choice. And that is the difference between the two viewpoints.

Ultimately, you will find that those who believe that something was always here and produced someone will live by luck; they will appeal to chance. They will say, "The best of luck to you." They will toss coins. They will read their horoscopes. They will do all kinds of things. And those who believe that someone produced something will say this universe is my home because this is my Dad's work. That is just the difference. So, it does have a bearing on your daily life. Do you understand me now?

I have jumped ahead a bit, but I want to show you how the difference of starting point will affect your life tomorrow morning. You will either get up and believe that you are in God's world, and he is in charge of it, and he is in charge of your life, and he has planned your life, and there is a providence that looks after you, or you will get up and you will say, "Well, I hope I have a good lucky day today." You either get up and you say, "Good morning, Lord," or "Good Lord, morning." And it goes right back to the choice you took at the beginning.

I made a little list of all the alternative views that are being thrown at me through the TV and through every other media. And I realised that Genesis 1:1 makes war on the whole lot. Here is the list – they are all *isms*. I am scared of those three little letters. When anything has an *i-s-m* at the end, a little bell jangles in me; all the *isms*. The only one I can feel happy about is baptism, but the rest, no.

But here they are: atheism says there is no God. Genesis 1:1 declares war on atheism, and says, "You're wrong. That's a lie."

Chapter 1: In the beginning

Agnosticism says, "I don't know if there's a God or not; there may be or there may not," and Genesis 1:1 declares war on that view and says, "You're wrong." Pantheism – some of these you may never have heard of, and you may be praying that you will never hear about them again. Well, you won't from me but just once. Pantheism says, "Everything is God; when I look at the trees, that's God." Genesis 1:1 declares war on that and says that those trees are creatures not the Creator.

Existentialism says, "God is my religious experience." Genesis 1:1 says, Wrong again. God existed long before there was anybody to have any religious experience. Rationalism says, "The only things that are true are the things that can be proved to my reason." Genesis 1:1 says, Wrong again. We declare war on that, because a thing is true whether you believe it or not if it's true. Humanism that says, "Man is God, man is the master of his fate, man is in charge, he's the highest creature." And Genesis 1:1 declares war on that view.

Materialism, common in the Western world, says, "Only matter is real, spirit is not real." Genesis 1:1 denies that. In the Eastern world it is mysticism that says, "Matter is not real but spirit is." And Genesis 1:1 says, No, spirit is real and matter is real. God created heavens and earth. Animism: that we are governed by spirits inhabiting this world. "Wrong again. God created heavens and earth." Polytheism: the belief that there are many gods. Hindus believe that there are three million gods. "Wrong." Genesis 1:1 declares war on that view. Dualism is a view that there are two gods, one good and one bad, and that is how you explain the world. You explain the good things by the good god and the bad things by the bad god, and Genesis 1 declares war on that view and says, "Wrong."

And finally, the most subtle of all, which is right inside the church: deism. And deism says, "I believe in God, in one God, and he created the world, but he can't control it so there are no miracles. He doesn't control the weather. Having wound it up

CREATION

like a clock it has to run by itself now, and therefore it runs on natural laws and God can do nothing about it anymore than I can. So, there's no point in praying about the weather tomorrow morning because God can't help it either." And deism is perhaps the most subtle of all these *isms* and it is found right through the Church, it really is. Genesis 1:1 says no, God not only created this world, he controls it, and miracles are possible every day because God is in charge of it.

Ultimately, there is only one *ism* that is left – it is called *theism*. And it is the opposite of atheism. Theism means that there is a God who is alive, active, who has made all this, who is in charge of it, who can do what he likes with any part of it, and he is still involved with it, and he is our God. He is the Father of the Lord Jesus Christ. And he is the God who controls the smallest part of our universe. He is a God who notices when a sparrow hops to the ground and who has counted the hairs of my head.

Whenever I read that text that not a sparrow falls to the ground, I thought it meant a sparrow having a coronary. Do you know what I mean? I thought of a poor little bird on a branch and keeling over and going thump, you know? And God saying, "Oh what a pity." Well, I have done a bit of searching the Greek since then, and I find out it is "Not a single sparrow hops to the ground without your Father knowing about it." That is the most ordinary thing that could happen that nobody would look at, and yet God was involved. Do you see the difference?

Now, against all those *isms*, against all those views which cover the majority of people in your town, if you really pin them down and ask them what kind of a God they really believe in you will find the majority are into those other views. It is only by the grace of God that you heard the truth: "In the beginning, God created the heavens and the earth." And you owe it to everybody in your town to convey that truth. You owe it to them not to leave them in delusion or in lies.

Now I am almost ready to expound the first verse of Genesis

Chapter 1: In the beginning

chapter one. That is the most sublime and the most comprehensive sentence in human language. As we begin to get into it, you will realise that this sentence is incredible. Everything hangs on it, and I just have the feeling that some of us take it for granted and never think about it enough. We assume it and rush on. But it is the most important thing perhaps that you can think about in this world. Everything else will fit into it. It says it all. And I want to tell you that you will not find that sentence anywhere else in the world.

Did you know that? Not another religion in the world has said that, not one. You can search all the scriptures, you can search the Quran, you can search the Holy Vedas, you can search all the scriptures of all the religions in the world and you will not find that sentence. You will not find it anywhere else but in this book. If you find it somewhere else it will be because someone is quoting this book. It is unique in all the writings of the human race. Only once has this ever been said.

So, let us look at it. "In the beginning," and that is a radical statement if ever there was one. We tend to read it as if it just says, "Once upon a time." Do you know what I mean? As if that is the beginning of the fairy tale. "Once upon a time." Most nice stories begin with that. But it is far more important than that. It is stating that our universe has not been around forever. And yet most people in our world and most men in history have believed the opposite, that the universe is eternal. I shall come back to that in a moment.

This is saying that this world in which we live is temporary and not permanent, and that is going to change your way of looking at it. It is not here forever, it has not been here forever, it will therefore not be a permanent home for anybody or anything; it is a temporary thing. Now that takes quite a bit of faith to accept that. You look at the mountains and the oceans and you say that is only temporary. It had a beginning and it will have an end. It has not always been there.

CREATION

Now I say that is revolutionary because I have been reading some of the Greek philosophers, and when you go back to the ancient Greeks you find that all of them believed that the universe has always been here in some form or other. Every evolutionist believes that the universe has always been here, either in terms of matter or energy, but something has always been here because nobody can grasp such a crazy notion as to believe that nothing became something all by itself. So, if you don't believe in someone, you have got to believe that something was always there. Do you follow me in that? I have never met anybody who believed that nothing could become something with no help. Therefore, once you cut out the Creator you cut out creation. Once you cut out the Originator you cut out origin. Do you follow me? Cut God out, and there cannot be a beginning.

I am sure you have heard of the Steady State and the Big Bang Theory. Have you? I wonder if I can explain that very simply, perhaps too simply for some who are scientifically educated. But you see, most scientists today are divided between those two schools. The majority vote is for the Big Bang. But among scientists, the Steady State and the Big Bang have been the two great theories about how our universe came to be the way it is. Let me tell you what they mean.

The Steady State was associated with an astronomer called Fred Hoyle. He said this: "Both, by the way, start from the knowledge we have, which seems established, that the universe is expanding. Every minute I speak the universe is bigger." I am prepared to accept that as fact; every indication seems to point that way. It could be proved wrong later. But I am going to accept that for the moment; that it is expanding, and they say it is expanding at a fifth of the speed of light. We are just in a universe that is shooting out from it.

So, they say, "Well, how did it come to be that way?" And the Steady State boys headed up by Fred Hoyle said, "Well, there must be matter being constantly created somewhere in the

Chapter 1: In the beginning

universe, perhaps in the black holes, that's sort of pushing in and therefore pushing it all out and filling up the spaces." Therefore, there is a constant creation of matter that is pushing it all out, and filling it all up. That is the Steady State Theory.

The Big Bang Theory is that once upon a time this universe was a tiny ball of such enormous pressure and density that it exploded, and it has been exploding ever since, and the dust that was caused by the explosion grouped together in planets here and planets there. Now I have simplified it, but I hope enough for you to grasp. These are the two theories we have to live with. If I can put it even more simply; one theory says we were blown up, with the emphasis on the blown, and the other that we were blown up with a steady continuous creation of new stuff.

But when you ask about these two theories, "But how did that little ball get there in the first place?" "Well, maybe before that the universe was contracting, and maybe before that it was expanding, and maybe it's in oscillation – getting small, big, small, big and it's been going on like that," the one thing they don't say is, "Well, there was nothing there before that little ball." The Steady State boys, you ask them, "Well, where is all that new matter coming from?" "Well, we're not sure. But we're sure something is producing it." And you will find that can't bear the thought that once upon a time there was nothing.

That is where the Bible cuts right across all other opinions. It says, "Once upon a time when nothing existed the God who was always there brought this universe into being." And on that we dare not shift one inch. Whatever battles we may get involved in they over evolution or over the six days in the warfare, a Christian says, "I'm not budging from the basic statement in this first verse that someone produced something, and it was the someone who was always there and not the something." As soon as you say the opposite – that something was always there and someone wasn't – do you know the ultimate end of that road? Instead of saying God created man in his own image you will finish up saying man created God in his own image.

These are the two paths. There are only two basic positions you can adopt in life: someone produced something or something produced someone. There is nothing in between. "In the beginning," it is a backwards prophecy. Do you know what I mean by that? Most prophecies go into the future, which we do not know and cannot possibly know, and a prophecy often tells you about the future that you could not possibly know. But this is a backwards prophecy, it tells you about the past that no one could know. There was no observer there, there was no reporter there, there was no one to write it down; unless there was someone there – God – who told us about it.

Therefore, Genesis 1 faces you with the choice: is this human speculation or divine revelation? And you will have to choose. Is this guess work or is it the only Person who was around telling us what he did? I see no other choice. So, right with the first verse you are faced with faith.

I remember God saying to Job, Were you there? Where were you when I laid the foundations of the earth? Where were you when I brought the snow? Where were you when I set the limits to the oceans? Where were you? And Job was humble enough to say, *Hole in one Lord, you got me. I wasn't there* [David Pawson's paraphrase!]. I think that kind of humility is called for when you approach Genesis 1. Instead of coming with all your theories to argue with God and try and prove that he is a liar, you come humbly and say, "God, you were there and I wasn't; that means I should come humbly to listen and to study."

Now the next word: "In the beginning, God," nothing else, a Person called God. The Bible does not try to prove his existence. It says if you are going to get anywhere in understanding the universe you will have to begin by believing in God. Not have to be argued into it, not have to be persuaded. In fact, the book of Hebrews says, "Whoever would come to God must first believe that he is." You will never find God if you don't believe

Chapter 1: In the beginning

that he is there. The very first step in understanding reality and understanding the truth about our universe is to start with the hypothesis that God is real. And that is scientific. Every scientific discovery is dependent on someone who had faith that it was there.

Pierre and Marie Curie believed that radium was there, and they found it was. A Jew believed that there must be another planet in our solar system that nobody knew about. It is only a few years since the last planet in our system was discovered, and it was because a Jew said, "There must be a planet somewhere there that is affecting the others. I believe it's there and I'm going to search for it until I find it," and he found it. And that is how we found the last planet in our solar system. It is not a bad way for scientists or Scripture students to start by believing it is there and looking for it.

Therefore, the Bible does not try and argue the existence of God. It just says, "In the beginning, God." Believe that and everything else will make sense. You do not have to explain God. You have to explain everything else. The existence of God is not a problem. It is the existence of this world that is the problem. It is the existence of me and my sin that is the problem; it is not the existence of God. So, the Bible does not bother with arguments about the existence of God, it just says, "In the beginning, God."

But what kind of a God? I began to make a list of everything Genesis 1 tells me about God. I found that not only did it mention him thirty-five times, but it told me many things about God. And for a bit of homework, I challenge you to get the list of things about him up to twenty by next week yourself. But I will give you a number of them, alright? What kind of a God is this who was always there? Who is the God we are dealing with, the God who made all that is?

The first is that he is a personal God: not it, but he. He has a mind that thinks and what a thought it was to produce this universe. He has got a will that decides to do something and then acts and does it, and he has got a heart that is really chuffed, if

CREATION

I may say so, with what he does. He looks at what he does and he says, "Oh boy, that's good, that's good. I did a good job on that. That's very good," and that is a Person with a heart. And if there is a mind, and a heart, and a will, that means he is a Person. We are not dealing with a force; we are dealing with a Person.

I remember when I did a programme on TV. And I spoke to one of the people I did it with and I said to them, "I've told you what I believe, now you tell me what you believe. Do you believe in God?" The person said, "Sort of." I said, "Well, what sort of?" This person replied, "Well, some *thing*, but not someone." Later as we were making the filming I was with that person and I said, "Lord, I want you to tell me something about that person that only you could know that will show that you know them and care for them."

As soon as I asked for that word of knowledge two words came into my mind, and they were such extraordinary words I couldn't believe they were true of the person. I just couldn't believe it was true. And that is when you feel you are walking a plank, and I thought if I say these words and they are not true, that will finish me off altogether. But I said them, and they were true. Months later that person said to me, "You know, that was the moment I began to believe in a personal God," because it was someone who knew, and who felt, who cared. The first thing Genesis 1 says about God to me is that I am dealing with a Person who thinks, and feels, and acts; someone I can understand, because I am a person too.

The second thing I found is that God is powerful. I will never forget when we were reading the story of creation to our children when they were smaller. My wife will remember – our eldest daughter, she just thought it through after we had read Genesis 1 and she said, "No sooner said than done." It just seemed a beautiful comment. In other words, God just has to say it and it is done. That is power.

You think of a man sitting at a big desk at the top of a large

Chapter 1: In the beginning

building in an office with plush carpet, you know, the man at the very top, and he just says, "Get that done." And he says it and it is done, he is powerful. In fact, you try and go to the man who has got enough power to get it done, don't you? You know he has just got to pick up a phone and say, "I'm sending someone down to you. See that he gets this," and you think, great. That is done because he said so, and he has got the power. And God is a powerful Person. He just has to say, "Let there be light," and there it is. He is personal and he is powerful.

What else does it tell me? It tells me he is a very orderly Person. Now, I would not like you to come into our home yet. We have not got it sorted out. We are in a mess. We are very conscious of it when people call. But you know, you go into some homes and they are so orderly. Do you ever notice? You almost don't like to sit down. Everything is ideal home exhibition, and you just sit on the edge of the chair hoping not to spoil the arrangement. You know the people living in that home are terribly orderly people, don't you? They like things just so.

Look at the top of a man's desk and you will find out what kind of a man he is. I am not going to develop this but just to point out that when I look at the order in the universe, the way in which things are so beautifully arranged, the way the insects fit the flowers, the way everything is in its place, the way things fit together – my God is a God who is orderly. Very mathematical too, that is another thing.

The next thing I notice is that God must be very creative. What an imagination he must have when you compare what we produce with what he produces. We can produce a million Volkswagen Beetles, but when you look at the beetles he produces, they are not all the same. It is not just the different colour, the shapes – I mean, who could think all these up? What an imagination, what a creative God he is. You are each unique. And God thought you up. He made it possible. What a creative Person.

I notice next that he is a singular person. There is only one

CREATION

God. What a relief that is, you know. If I believed in three million gods, I would be worried all day about which one I had upset. That is the trouble with polytheism. You don't know which one you are dealing with if you believe in many gods. What a relief it is to know that there is only one God. That is why it is a universe because it is a uni-God who made the universe, and there is only one God we have to deal with. Not two, not three, not five, not three million, just one; but having said that, Genesis 1 tells us that he is actually a plural God. The word in Genesis 1:1 actually has an "s" on the end. "In the beginning, Gods created." In the Hebrew its Elohim, which is plural; but the verb "created" is singular.

Now here is a mystery, God has a plural name and yet singular verb. Then later on he says, "Let us". Is that a kind of royal "we" like the Queen? "We have decided to create man." Now there is a mystery here, and in the rest of the Bible we will find out what that mystery is. It is a lovely mystery that God is a family; Father, Son, and Spirit. I wonder if that gets you excited. It gets me excited because it means that love existed before the universe. Because if God was only one Person all alone, he could not be love, because love is something you can only have with someone else, and it means that love was always there. Before any matter was created, love was there. God is plural as well as singular.

Next, he is distinct from creation. He was there before he created the universe, and he rested from it afterwards and had nothing to do with it for a day, and had a day off. That is terribly important because you must never get nature and God confused. Some people give nature a capital "n," and think that is God. They worship nature. But God is quite separate from nature. He made it, but he is quite apart from it. He can control it but he is not identified with it.

Oh, a lovely thing now. Genesis 1 tells me that the God who made all this is good. I love that phrase. Whenever I am asked to give a title for a meeting somewhere, I am hopeless at thinking

Chapter 1: In the beginning

of it months or a year beforehand. And they want to advertise the title, so I always say, "Good God", and that covers everything. I can speak on anything I like under that heading because it really does cover everything. I remember going to a university in New Zealand; they had a big poster up and it just had a horrible photograph of me, it really was. It was a suit and whitewashed, a dreadful photograph of me glaring out of the middle. It just had a face, the date, the time, lecture theatre B, and then underneath it said, "Good God."

The lecture theatre was packed with students, and we had three days, and oh, it was super. There were real conversions, but anyway, it started with that. But it really does cover all my theology – good God. Genesis 1 puts those two words together. I am afraid I don't like hearing people use those two words because they have read something that surprises them, because those are the two most precious words "Good", "God." That means that everything he touches is good, everything he makes is good, and everything that is good brings him pleasure and pleases him. He likes to see good things because he is a good God.

Next, he is like us. That is an amazing thought. I would have thought that God would be so unlike me I would never understand him. But he is like me. I have got two hands, and God understands that because the Bible talks about the hand of God. I have got two eyes, and the Bible talks about the eye of God. I have got nostrils and I can smell nice things, and smell a stink as well, and it says of God that something stinks in his nostrils. I have got ears and he has got an ear and he can hear. I have got a mouth and I can talk, and he talks. I have got an arm, and his arm is laid bare. It talks about his kidneys, the deepest feelings that he has; feelings deep down for us. The Book talks about the feet of God. Now, does that mean he has a body? No, we are told that he is Spirit. But it means that every physical function is like him because he can do it without a body, the same thing. But that means he is like me.

CREATION

So, when I make a thing with my hands – and I love making things with my hands – it is such a change from preaching, you can see where you have been, you can see what you have done straight away. I love making things with my hands. I think that is how God feels. He is just like that. When I have done a good job and made something in the garden that is satisfying, I stand back. I get a real kick out of that, do you? God is just like that. He saw what he had made and he was so thrilled.

Next, he is unlike us, because there are some things that he does in Genesis that I have never done and never will do. Somebody once said to me, "Have you ever been tempted to turn stones into bread?" I said, "No, that's not one of my temptations." That is the sort of temptation that would come to the Son of God, not to me. So, he is unlike us as well as like us.

The next one is that he wants to reproduce himself. Did you want to have children? So does he. Did you want to see new life that you had brought into being? I will never forget the day I looked at our firstborn. Many of you know that moment. It is an incredible moment. There they are like a little, skinny rabbit, and I can't say they are attractive as soon as they are born. But you look at them and you think, "Gosh, we created that. We've reproduced ourselves." God is like that.

Next, he is alive, which means that he is active, he is doing things, he is busy.

Finally, he is a communicator. He loves to talk to others, always talking. Genesis 1 is full of him saying things, communicating. Do you realise that if God were not a communicator, then we would not know much about him at all? I would not know how the world began if he had not been a talker. The world would never have come to be if he had not been a talker. God is a communicator. O Lord, thank you that you are a God who talks, that you speak, that you put your thoughts into words and communicate.

Let us move on, "In the beginning, God created," created. There are two words used in this chapter of what God did at

Chapter 1: In the beginning

the beginning: "created" and "made." And I want to tell you the difference between those two words. It is an important difference. The biggest is that "made" is used of man in the rest of the Bible. Noah *made* an ark, the Hebrew slaves in Egypt *made* bricks, Bezalel *made* the tabernacle. But never, never once does the rest of the Bible say a man "created" anything. Now that is unlike modern English. We talk about a great piece of music as a marvellous creation or a work of art as a marvellous creation, but the Bible never talks like that. It keeps these two words, one for God and the other for God and man. That is going to be rather important.

Let us take the word "make" first. The word "make" means very simply to manufacture. It is a craft word; it means to take a piece of wood and make a lectern out of it. That is "to make" and that is something that all of us can do, whether you make an apple pie or whether you make a chair or whatever you make, you have taken some material and changed its form and you have made something. That is something that you can do, and it is something that God does as well. And a lot of the things in Genesis 1 he made. He took the material that was already there and he made something else and he changed its form, its shape, he made it.

But that is only one word in Genesis 1. There is another that is used very sparingly. It is only used three times, and that is the word "created", the Hebrew word *barra* where "make" is the Hebrew word *asa*. Now, *asa* means "make" which we can do, *barra* means "create" which no man can ever do. So, what is the difference? Let us try and feel our way into it. First of all, let us realise that the word "make" must have a person involved. The wood would never change into a pulpit without a person doing it. Do you follow what I mean?

So, even the word "make" means that no part of this universe could have arrived by itself; no part, none of the flowers, none of the birds, none of the animals, nothing could have arrived without God being involved. So, the whole idea that somehow

CREATION

matter became life and life turned into different species – that is rubbish if you mean by that that it could do that without God. Now true, God could have taken something that existed and changed it into something else, and that would be making it. But it could not have happened without him. Do you follow me?

So, the word "make" could allow a certain amount of what we call evolution in which one thing became something else but not without God. Do you follow me? It could not have happened naturally. It could only have happened supernaturally, and there we part company with most evolutionists. Even if we allow that some animals changed into other animals, we have to say that could not have happened without God. It therefore did not happen by chance, it happened by choice because God chose to make it that way. Do you follow me? That is the first thing I want to say about "make".

Now about "create" I want to say something else. To create is something we can't understand because we can't do it. I have never created anything in my life, nor will I ever, because to create means to make something so new that it was not there before – not in any shape or form, it was not there. It is a new departure. It is something that not only could not have happened without personal intervention, but it could not have happened without supernatural, personal intervention, without a miracle, without God putting something totally new into the situation that was not there before. Now, making things, you make them of what was there before. Creating things, you make them of what was not there before. Do you follow me on that?

The three times Genesis 1 talks about creation are these: matter, life, and man. At those three points God was not making, he was creating. All the other points he was refashioning what was already there, but at these points he was putting something in that had not been there; something so new that only he could produce out of nothing what is now here. And I find it interesting that *man* is one of those three things, life and matter the other

Chapter 1: In the beginning

two. That means that nothing became something by creation, then God made it into something. Do you follow?

He created matter then he made it and refashioned it. Then he created life and refashioned it: animal, plant, bird life, and refashioned it. Then he created man. Now, that tells me that at those three points not only did something happen that could not have happened without personal intervention, but something happened that was totally new, that had just not existed before. Here we part company almost totally with the evolutionists, who believe that matter, which was always there, changed into life by itself and ultimately changed into man. We just cannot go along with that. God is telling us utterly clearly, "Yes, I did manufacture some things; I did take what was already there and change it. But man was something that wasn't there, and life was something that wasn't there, and matter was something that was not there." Now, that is where I stand on the Bible.

So, it allowed for the refashioning, even allowing for the refashioning within plants, bird, and animal life that God says he did. It does say that the end product of his refashioning was species that would remain true to type and could only reproduce themselves. So that his refashioning, which he caused, which from one point of view might be called evolution, from an observer's point of view nevertheless produced species that could only reproduce themselves after their kind. So, suppose he did change a cat into a dog, supposing he did it. It does not say he did, but suppose. That would fit in with the Scripture, if the scientist proves that that happened. He has not actually, the scientist. But supposing he did, then that would not worry me because the cat could not have turned into a dog without God's refashioning. And after he had refashioned them, the cat could never breed a dog and the dog could never breed a cat. So, they were distinct, each after its kind. I hope you are following me here.

We are going to say more about that in the next chapter but that is what I understand by "created", to add something so new, which was not there before, that only God could do it. Man can manufacture. I suppose that most of the flowers in your garden have been made by man. Very few flowers in your garden were as they were created by God. They have been bred and crossbred and hybridised – your hybrid tea roses. Man has made those. But he has not created them, he has made them. But he has never made a rose into a dog. He has bred all kinds of dogs, but he has never made a dog into a monkey. So, are you beginning to get the feel of what Genesis is saying? It is clear, it is simple.

Certain things God made out of materials that were already there. But when he changed them, it fixed them and they only reproduce after their kind. Certain things he created that were not there before. Matter was not there – he made it; life was not there – he created it; man was not there – we are a creation. I want to tell you something. You are not a monkey. You are created in the image of God. Never regard yourself as an animal or you might behave like one. Tell kids in the classroom that they came from the jungle and they will go back to it as soon as they leave school, and you cannot blame them if they behave like animals when you have told them that is what they are.

"As a man thinks in his heart so *is* he." If he thinks he is an animal he will behave like one. If he thinks he came from the jungle then he will behave as if he is in a jungle. If he thinks he arrived through the survival of the fittest, then the survival of the fittest will be his rule of life. Whether it is Hitler and his fascism or trade unionism gone wild, the toughest will get the money. The toughest will get the country; it is survival of the fittest. And Hitler built his state on that belief, on Darwinism. Did you know that? That is why he called his book, *My Struggle*. He got the word "struggle" from Darwin's book, which is full of the word "struggle" (the struggle to survive). So, Hitler wrote *Mein Kampf*, that is where it came from. You see, we are dealing with big things here. What you believe about your beginning will determine how you behave right now.

Chapter 1: In the beginning

Well, let me finish this verse and then we are through, "The heavens and the earth." "In the beginning". So there was a beginning when there was nothing and something arrived, but not by itself – someone put it there. "In the beginning, God created," brought into being what was not there before, "the heavens and the earth." Both these words are what I call elastic words. They tend to have a double meaning, and they still do in modern English. "Heaven" – we tend to talk about the birds in heaven, meaning the sky. And then the word extends to cover outer space, and then it becomes a plural word, "the heavens" – you find that in the Bible. You find "heaven" refers to the sky, our atmosphere and then "the heavens" refers to what we call outer space. So that is why I called it that in my paraphrase. "The heavens" means everything in outer space.

"Earth" also has a double meaning. I am trying to dig our front garden and get it shipshape. I was surprised; the earth is quite good. There is some good earth there. So, I use it as a soil in my garden. You say, "You know, that looks like a good bit of earth," or "Let's earth it," or when we bury someone, "Earth to earth" – back to the soil. So, we use the word "earth" of the land, but we also use it of the whole planet. So did the Hebrews. Sometimes they used the word *ha-aretz*, land, as the land of Israel. Sometimes they used it as the whole planet.

So, "the heavens and the earth" means everything in outer space and everything on planet Earth. That is what God brought into being and it was not there before. There was nothing there before, and our God brought it into being. I almost just want to worship at that point. When I think of the size of the universe, which we are now beginning to realise – our little earth is just under eight thousand miles across. If you dig straight through from here to Australia you will dig through eight thousand miles. That is the size of our earth. Well, that is pretty big. Our galaxy is about one hundred thousand light years across. So, if you went on a journey through our galaxy at the speed of light it would take you one hundred thousand years just to get through our galaxy. And that galaxy is one of many others.

I am sure you know that our universe is a sphere, it is a ball, it is round. Almost everything in this world, in the universe is round. Planet Earth is round, the sun is round. The universe is a great big bubble, it is round and getting bigger every minute; it is a round bubble. How far is that across? Well, I have looked it up. It is 15,600 million light years across. I can't understand that. I just can't grasp it, and yet that is what God created.

Somebody once asked me, "Where is God in the universe?" I said, "Wrong question." They said, "What do you mean?" I said, "You should have asked me, where is the universe in God?" Because what you make is always less than yourself. Just think, *that* God made planet Earth, and from that word onward, Genesis 1 is entirely concerned with this little planet, and the rest of the Bible is concerned with this little planet. I find that amazing. And our galaxy is right at one side of the universe. Within our galaxy the sun is two-thirds from the centre to the circumference, so it is right on one side. We are right on one side of the sun, and God says, planet Earth is the centre of the universe to me. And the Bible is what is called geocentric or earth-centred. You say, "That's crazy. We're right on the edge of the universe, of our galaxy, of the sun. We're right in one little corner here," and God says not to me you're not.

There are signs all around Basingstoke to the town centre, but if you look on a map it is not exactly the centre. The centre is some way away from here. But in fact, all the sign posts point to here, the town centre, or a little bit further down the road where the shops are, because that is where it all happens. And the centre of the universe to God is not the pinpoint in the middle of that bubble. Way over here, that is the centre, and everything actually revolves around that, not the planets. We revolve around the sun but everything God has planned revolves around this little speck of dust. As far as we know, it is the only place where

Chapter 1: In the beginning

there is life, the only place where there is the temperature and enough water, and it is in a very, very thin layer – so thin that if I went thirty miles up that way or thirty miles down that way, I would be a goner unless I was in a space craft or something. But you and I live in this tiny thin wafer, around one little speck of interstellar dust.

And God says that it is the most important place in the universe to him. He said to his Son that it was where he wanted him to go, and it as where they were going to work out the whole future of the universe. My new heaven and earth, we'll work it out on that little planet. That's where I'm going to put people. So, when I read modern astronomy I get all lost. I think where am I? Help, who am I? I'm nothing. And then I read my Bible again. "In the beginning, God created the heavens," and I would have understood if it had stopped there. God created the universe; this great God made everything that is. I would have understood if it had stopped there. But suddenly it said, "and the earth." That is where I come into the picture. Well, I feel we have said quite enough in this chapter. We will pick up the rest of Genesis 1 in the next chapter and we will see just how God set about it, and what he tells us about our world, and above all, about man himself. Who are we? What is it all about?

CHAPTER 2:

THE SEVEN DAYS OF CREATION

I now want to look at the rest of Chapter 1 without touching on the creation of man. I am looking at what Genesis 1 says about the world and I want to introduce it by looking at the style and the structure of the chapter to see how God communicates to us things that otherwise we would never know. We shall look at the medium. Then we are going to look at the passage itself and look at the one subject, the few verbs and the many objects in that chapter. And then we are going to look at some of the problems of science and Scripture. And there are three major ones – The *sequence* of creation: Is the order in Genesis the order that science agrees with or not? The *speed* of creation: was it 6x24 hour days or billions of years? There is a slight discrepancy between science and Scripture there. And the major one – What was the *principle* of selection: was it natural or supernatural?

So, these are the three major issues. And then we will just conclude by looking at the message that is conveyed through all this, which very simply is we live in an orderly universe because it was ordered. And that is the real message of Genesis 1 about the world in which we live.

I want to read now a paraphrase of Genesis 1. I debated whether to read the normal biblical version or a paraphrase but you probably know the biblical version fairly well so the paraphrase might bring it freshly to you, but you will see how much better the normal versions are when we discuss it later. But let me read the paraphrase:

"A long time ago when nothing else existed, the God who

CREATION

had always been there brought into being the entire universe; everything in space including this planet. At first the earth came into being as a mass of fluid matter uninhabitable and uninhabited. It was shrouded in darkness and engulfed in water. God's own Spirit was fluttering just above the flood. Then God commanded, 'Let light in' and there it was. It looked just right to God but he decided to alternate light with darkness, giving them different names, day and night. The original darkness and this new light were the evening and morning of God's first working day.

"Then God spoke again, 'Let there be two reservoirs of water with an expanse between them,' so he separated the water on the surface from the moisture in the atmosphere and that is how the sky, as God called it, came to be. This was his second day's work on creation.

"The next thing God said was, 'Let the surface water be concentrated in one area so that the rest may dry out.' Sure enough, it happened. From then on, God referred to sea and land separately. He liked what he saw and said, 'Now let the land sprout vegetation, plants with seed and trees with fruit, all able to reproduce themselves.' And they appeared. All kinds of plants and tree, each able to propagate its own species. Everything was fitting into God's plan. His third day's work was over.

"Now God declared, 'Let different sources of light be visible in the sky. They will distinguish days from nights and make it possible to measure seasons, special days and years but their main purpose will be to provide illumination.' And so it is just as he said. The two brightest lights are the larger sun that dominates the day and the lesser moon that predominates in the night sky, surrounded by the twinkling stars. God put them all there for earth's sake to light it, to regulate it, and to maintain the alternating pattern of light and darkness. God was pleased that his fourth day's work had turned out so well.

"The next order God issued was, 'Let the sea and the sky teem with animated creatures – with shoals of swimming fish

Chapter 2: The seven days of creation

and flocks of flying birds.' And God brought into being all the species that inhabit the oceans, from the huge monsters of the deep to the tiny organisms floating in the waves; and all the variety of birds and insects on the wing in the wind above. To God it was a wonderful sight and he encouraged them to breed and increase in numbers so that every part of sea and sky might swarm with life. That ended his fifth day.

"Then God announced, 'Now let the land also teem with living creatures – mammals, reptiles and wildlife of every sort.' As before, no sooner was it said than it was done. He made all kinds of wildlife, including mammals and reptiles, each as a distinct type. And they all gave him pleasure. At this point, God reached a momentous decision: 'Now let us make some quite different creatures, more our kind, human beings just like us. They can be in charge of all the others, the fish in the sea, the birds of the air and the animals on the land.' To resemble himself God created mankind to reflect in themselves his heart, will and mind to relate to each other, male and female entwined. Then he affirmed their unique position with words of generous encouragement: 'Produce many offspring for you are to occupy and control the whole earth – the fish in the sea, the birds of the air and the animals on the land are all yours to master. I am also giving you seed-bearing plants and fruit-bearing trees as your food supply. The birds and the beasts can have the green leaves for their food,' and so it was. God surveyed everything he had made and he was very satisfied. It was all so right, so beautiful, six days' work well done.

"Outer space and planet Earth were now complete in all their vastness and variety. Since nothing more was needed, God took a day off. This is why he designated each seventh day as a special day, set apart from the others as a day for himself alone because on that day he was not busy with what had been his daily work. That is how our universe was born and came to be the way it is."

Well, unfamiliar words can make it a little fresher to us.

CREATION

Do you realise that those words we have read, this chapter we are studying is either a fraud or a miracle? It is written as an eyewitness account. It is written in the form of someone who was actually there and saw it happen. Now, since it is absolutely impossible for a human being to have been present and made a report, it is either due to human invention or divine inspiration – there is no other choice. It is either total guesswork and speculation or it is the truth because there was *one* eyewitness; there was one Person who saw it happen and seven times it says "And God saw..."

Now, that is the choice and the basic decision everybody has to make with the first page in the Bible is – Is that a human invention or divine inspiration? Because there is no middle ground, it is either one or the other. And I am going to exercise faith and assume that God was there and that he was an eyewitness and that he is describing it exactly as it was. "He made known his ways to Moses," said one of the Psalms, which means that God had to communicate what happened to us and that faces him with a problem. It is always a problem when I am preparing these talks, I am constantly thinking, how can I best present this to you in words that you will understand, in thought forms you can grasp, in pictures you can see. And I have constantly got to be thinking of you, not just of the study, not just of the chapter but of you, if I am going to communicate things to you.

And therefore, you have to adapt your style to the people you are talking to. Now frankly, if I were giving a lecture, as I did in Aberdeen to theological students in the Church of Scotland College there, I would use rather different language. And you see God had this problem.

Winston Churchill had the problem during World War II. Winston Churchill had a better grasp of the English language than almost anybody I know. When he wrote books, he used a total of 25,000 words. That was his vocabulary; whereas ordinary folk use 5,000 words during our lifetime. So, when Winston

Churchill prepared his speeches for the radio, he cut out 20,000 of his words and he just spoke in the 5000 words that he knew we used. So, he would say things like: "I have nothing to offer you but blood, tears, toil and sweat" and "Never was so much owed by so many to so few," and about Hitler's threat to wring this chicken's neck, he just said, "Some chicken! Some neck!" And he deliberately simplified his language, his style. If you read his books, he was a master of English grammar. When somebody split an infinitive in the House of Commons he said, "That is an example of extremely bad English up with which I will not put." And he could do that, but when he spoke to us ordinary folk, he communicated in language we could understand.

Now here is God and he is wanting to communicate the story of his creation and he is not communicating it to another god because there isn't one. He is communicating the story to one part of his creation, for human beings are the only part of his creation that will read this story or know where they came from. So, he had to adapt his style to us and therefore he simplified the whole story, almost to the point of distortion, so that he could write it in a form that would be understood by all men and women in all time and in all space. And the reason I am emphasising this is that you must not expect this to be a scientific statement. If he had put it in scientific language then we would have had to wait until the twentieth century before anyone would have understood it. Do you follow me?

And a lot of the arguments spring from that simple misunderstanding that he wrote this chapter for ordinary people in all time, in all space – so he had to make it utterly simple. And you know, he only uses 76 different words to tell us the whole thing. And they are all words which you will find in every language on the earth. Now, isn't that remarkable? Now, in my paraphrase I just gave you I used nearly 300 words and it would have to be rewritten almost every generation so now you see why it was such a poor alternative. Do you follow me?

CREATION

I wrote that for you but if I were somewhere else, I would have to rewrite that thing. But God was going to write it just once for everybody so he only used 76 words and every man on earth has known what the sky is and what the land is and what the sea is and what the birds are and what the fish are – these are common concepts to the entire human race. You know, already as I read this chapter it has got the stamp of a divine Author. It always takes a very great brain to make something simple. Have you noticed that? It is the half-experts who use the big words, have you noticed that too? The great men can always spell it out simply for you.

Somebody once asked Albert Einstein, "Explain to me the relativity of time." Now, then, a lesser man could have really dressed it up in scientific terms. Do you know what Albert Einstein said? He said, "When I'm with a pretty girl two hours seems like a minute but when I'm sitting on a hot stove one minute it seems like two hours." And that was all he said, and in utterly simple terms that anybody could understand he explained the relativity of time. And that was the man that worked out the riddles of the universe.

Well now, if a great *man* can spell out things simply then it would take a really great God to write the story of creation in language that any man anywhere could grasp. So don't expect scientific language. That word *kind* for example, it does not actually mean species. It just means kind. Do you follow me? And so, in vegetation, God says there are three kinds – there are little plants and he calls it grass. And then he said there are bigger ones and he calls them herbs and then there are bigger ones called trees, and those are the only three kinds that he mentioned. So don't think he is talking about species or genre or phyla or all those other scientific terms, he is just speaking about different kinds.

When he talks about the animals, he mentions three kinds – domesticated, game and wildlife; and every man knows those

Chapter 2: The seven days of creation

three kinds of animals – the animals you keep yourself, the animals you hunt and kill for food and the other animals that you never have anything to do with; three kinds of animals and every man understands those three kinds. So, you see you must not expect a scientific treatise here. It is utterly simple to convey the truth that God wanted to convey and that was – I did it, every bit of it; it is an orderly world you live in because I ordered it that way. That is the truth. And I marvel at the way he has done it. There is even more to it than that. He actually tells us the story from the point of view of someone standing on the earth at the time. What condescension, that God up in heaven should tell us the story as if he were standing on the earth and what it looked like from there; so that the sun is up, you know? And he can use human language like sunrise and sunset. And we know the sun does not rise and we know it does not set. It is the world spinning round, but he said, I'll look at it your way so you can understand. And so, we speak about the stars up in the sky. They are not up to God. In fact, the Psalms – one of the Psalms – says that God has to bend down to look at the stars. Now wasn't it lovely of him to talk to us about the stars up in the sky. He is saying it from our point of view and we shall see that that will answer a number of things.

So, the scientists can say, "Well, it's ridiculous talking about the stars up in the sky, they're not up. And it's ridiculous to talk about the sun rising; it doesn't rise." Well, we will leave the scientist with his quibbles and I will just go on talking about the sun rising, won't you? And thank God that he does not get all wrapped up in scientific jargon. Otherwise, he would leave most of us standing. With utterly short, simple sentences like "And God saw that it was good" you hardly need to get past primary English to receive that, and yet it is all there.

The next thing I would like to talk about is the structure of this chapter; it is quite unique. It is remarkable how beautifully put together the story is, easily remembered. It is given to us in

CREATION

the form of seven days and we will just forget the seventh for a moment because that was his day off and we will look at the six days. And again, it is so beautifully put together. There are three days and three days, and before he tells us what he did on those two lots of three days, he says the earth was without form and void. It was just a mass of matter with no features and no life. And so, in the first three days he set about making it habitable. He set about giving it features and instead of it just being a formless mass he began to divide one thing from another – light from darkness on the first day; the sea from the sky on the second day; the land from the oceans on the third day. And in those three days he was getting the home ready. He was forming an environment where life was possible and those three things have not happened on any other planet in the universe. It is the only one he has made habitable.

To God, this is the centre of the universe, as I said in the previous chapter. And so, he spent three days getting the house ready and then another three days filling it with particular inhabitants. And so, the earth that was without form now had form and the earth that was empty was now full. And he filled every part of it; every part that he had made he filled with particular creation. So, can you see the beautiful order? You could write it out, you could memorise it. So simply – three days to get the place ready, three days to fill it up. So, he separated light from darkness and then he put the sun and the moon and the stars there. So, he separated the sea from the sky and put that vital atmosphere in between. And by the way, that came about because the gas which was in the molten rock was released and separated the moisture into two sorts of moisture – water on the surface and clouds in the sky. And that vital atmosphere which is so thin… I never cease to marvel when I am flying at how thin, how wafer-thin, that shield is in which we live safely which shields us from heat and cold and which enables us to breathe. And it is only a few miles deep – wafer thin compared to the size of the earth. But God had to make that atmosphere because he wanted us in there.

And then he separated land from sea. So, into the sea and the sky, when he had separated those, later he put birds in the air and fish in the sea, literally to multiply by the millions, to fill every part of that thing with life. And then, when he had created the land and the sea, again by a process of separating out the wet from the dry, then he could put animals and men in there later. It is so orderly, isn't it? It is so logical; it is so simple. I am not going to deal with the problems right now. I want you to grasp the basic order and simplicity of it before we deal with the problems because some people get far too bogged down in the problems before they have grasped the beauty of it, and seen the order of it and what God is saying.

There is also a unique mathematical feature in this chapter – everything is in threes, sevens or tens, which tells you that God is very mathematical. And that goes right the way through the Bible you will find. God has a mathematical mind, a tidy mind. If you are mathematically inclined, you will have a tidy, analytical mind and you will like things nicely like this. God is very mathematical. I mean, take the threes – well, there are three days to get it ready and three days to fill it up. Three times he creates something – matter, life and man. When he gets to man, the word "created" is used three times for man. Three times he names things, three times he blesses things, three times he makes things; it is all in threes. And we shall find in a moment that God himself is in threes – in the very first verse. Isn't that amazing? I will explain that in a moment.

Sevens – seven times God saw what he had made and had a good look at it. Seven times he said, that's good. The whole thing was completed in seven days. The first verse in Hebrew is just seven words and you will find that seven is just one of God's favourite numbers. It is a kind of nice round number to him. It is a perfect number, it is a complete number. And you

CREATION

will find that it is in sevens. You don't find things in twos or in fives here. It is all in threes and sevens, and the other one is in tens. That is a favourite number of God, especially when he is doing some talking. And he loves to give ten commandments. And before ever he gave the Ten Commandments to Moses, he gave ten commandments to creation. Ten times "God says".

So, God is a very orderly Person. He likes things tidy; he likes things neat. But he does not like things uniform; he loves variety. So, he likes order but he likes variety, and we are going to see in a moment that is very relevant to the discussion of evolution. God is a God who loves order and loves variety. He likes everything in its place but he loves everything to be different. And so, he created this world in a way that meant he would have unity and variety but not uniformity. And evolution could not have produced that.

In all this there is a total contrast to all the other religions of the world. You will have to take my word for this, but recently scholars have dug up the other accounts of creation in other religions. They have found the Babylonian account of creation. You read them – they are so different from Genesis 1 that the silly idea that Moses was copying it from Babylon is just crazy. Those other stories, there is no order in them, they are full of flowery speech, they are full of obscure metaphors and figures of speech. This is the only one that is a straight, simple, orderly account and it is unique.

Now let us look at the passage before the problems. It is full of very simple sentences; and if I can just give you a little reminder about grammar, a sentence is basically made up of three parts – a subject, a verb and an object. And the verb normally has to agree with the subject, so if the subject is singular the verb has to be singular. If the subject is plural the verb has to be plural. And God breaks the grammatical rule straight away because there is not a single verb that agrees with the subject in any sentence in this chapter. Now that is a bit of a shock, and it should in Hebrew

Chapter 2: The seven days of creation

and in Greek and in every other language. But it doesn't here, and we are going to learn something very surprising.

So, let us look at the one subject; there is one subject to every sentence – God, God, God, God – every sentence he is the subject, he starts it all off. He initiates everything that happens. Each of the verbs in Hebrew uses the singular form - but the subject, 'God', is in the plural form. This is lost in the English where the verb is the same whether 'I make' singular or 'We make' - plural ... in English it is the same word 'make'. Now, does that stretch your imagination a little? Well, let us look at the subject first; it is God and there is a unique name for God used here, Elohim, Elohim, E-l-o-h-i-m; and that is not a singular word, it is a plural word. And there are three sorts of Hebrew noun that you can have – one is singular and it means one, then there is another form, which is dual, that means two and then there is another form that is plural, which means at least three.

Now, in English we usually just have singular and plural, which means two and more, but the Hebrews had 1, 2, and then 3 or more. And Elohim is three; now isn't that amazing? You could almost translate it: "In the beginning Gods created", and it is plural and it means three. In the very first sentence we encounter the Trinity – remarkable, isn't it?

Is there any trace of the three Persons who make up the Godhead in the rest of Genesis 1? Yes, there is when you look. Just a verse or two later you hear about the Spirit of God and there Is the second one coming into the picture. And you know that there are at least two because later on a sentence begins: "Let *us* make man..." so somebody else is around there. And in a more subtle way – and here I think you would need to read the New Testament as well to get the whole picture – between God and his Spirit there is a Word passing to and fro; there is a Word between them. I don't know if you thought that God spoke to nothing. I used to think that until I read my Bible a bit more carefully. I thought when God said, "Let there be light"

CREATION

he was just either speaking to himself or speaking to nothing. Did you think that? But when you read Genesis 1 carefully, he was speaking to his Spirit. He was giving orders to his Spirit.

The Spirit was waiting for those orders, hovering over the chaos, waiting to shape it, waiting to do something about it. In fact, the literal word is, "The Spirit was *fluttering* over the flood" because the earth was just a fluid mass of matter. It was all liquid and it was covered with water and it was dark. And the Spirit was fluttering just over the earth. That is the literal word – fluttering. And it only occurs one other time in the first five books of the Bible and that is in a place in Deuteronomy where it says, "As the mother eagle flutters over her nest" to stir it up and get them flying – it is the same word. In other words, fluttering to do something underneath, to move the situation. It is a vivid picture of the Spirit of God saying, right, I'm ready to move this lot. I'm ready to get them flying, I'm ready to do something. And he is waiting for orders. Does that get you excited? Now you know who God the Father is talking to.

And God says, let the light in. The Spirit says, right. And it is done. The Spirit of God is the executive of God; he gets things done. That is why it was the Spirit of God who convicted you of sin. It was the Spirit of God who brought you to the new birth. It is the Spirit of God who does what God the Father tells him needs doing. That is why we need the Holy Spirit to do the work of God, because he does what God says.

And so, between them a Word is passing. Now, to us a word is usually simply an expressed thought, it is a sound, but the Bible says that when God speaks it is more than just a sound. The Word is actually a Person, it says that that God's method of communication is a Person, and if you want to follow this through, you read the first few verses of John's Gospel: "In the beginning was the Word and the Word was with God and the Word was God," and then it says, "without him was not anything made that has been made." Without the Word of God nothing was

Chapter 2: The seven days of creation

made that has been made, and the Word was the link between God the Father and his Spirit.

Now are you beginning to see something? And if you want one other passage to read, then Colossians chapter 1 and verses 15 to 17 is another that picks up this idea. And it says that through Christ all these things came into being. Jesus, the Son of God, is the Word, the communication between God and his Spirit. So right now, the subject of chapter 1 is Father, Son and Spirit; the Trinity is right there at creation, all three of them. But they are so united and so in harmony in all they do that God uses singular verbs. In the beginning Gods created, plural, singular. Three, one. I just find that amazing. What human author inventing this would have thought of doing that? This must come from God. I am sorry, there is no alternative. It really must come from the only Person who knew what was going on. "In the beginning God [three] created [one]". And three in perfect harmony – it is closer than triplets; that is why we have had to coin the word Tri-unity, or Trinity. Because we needed something even closer than three people like each other.

Well, that is the subject. And when God said, let's make man, I just see the three of them getting together and saying, let's do something that's really special. And it is at that point that they burst into poetry. The only verse in the whole chapter that is in poetry is when they decide to make man. And the reason is that whenever the Bible speaks in prose it is speaking to your head but when it is speaking poetry it is speaking to your heart. Most prophecy comes in poetry, by the way, which is intriguing.

Now let us look at the few verbs. And I just recall what I said in the last chapter – that there is a difference between *created* and *made*. *Made* is a verb that is applied to man in the rest of the Old Testament. *Created* never is. And *created* means to bring such new things into the situation that a fundamentally new thing has happened that would never have happened from the situation itself. Whereas to make something is to take what

CREATION

is already there and change its shape. And God produced the creation with a combination of totally new – fundamentally new – radical departures, *and* by developing what was already there. So, there is room for *some* evolution, but not for total evolution. Do you follow me in that?

But he had to bring some totally new things in. And the three points at which he had to do something totally new were matter, life and man. And none of those things would have arrived if God had not interjected something radically new into the situation. But in between, it says, he made, he made, he made. He was taking something already there, changing it; taking something, changing it. Scientists would talk about mutation. I prefer the words *creation* and *made*. But those are the two verbs, all in the singular.

There is the verb *said*, which we have looked at, the ten commandments of creation, singular. There is the verb *saw*, singular, but it is always "And Gods" saw that it was good. And then there is the word *blessed*. The first chapter of the Bible includes blessed. I am so thrilled about that. God did not just *make us*, he wanted to bless from the beginning. He blessed the animals and he blessed us. He blessed the birds and the fish. And I had to ask, well, what does blessing mean, if you can bless animals? How do you bless them? And do you know I came to the conclusion that the basic meaning of the word *bless* is to enable you to have more of what you have got that is good. Now that is a very simple definition. If you have got something really good, to bless you is to give you more of it. Do you follow me? So, he blessed the animals and he said, now multiply and have more. And if he blesses the church, he will give you more people. And if you have found joy in the Lord, if he blesses you he will give you more joy. Do you follow?

Blessing is to multiply what is good that is already there. And so, God said, I bless you; now fill the earth. And when I looked up some of the figures, like a cod has 150 million eggs, I thought boy, that's some blessing. The potential. When I consider that

Chapter 2: The seven days of creation

millions of tonnes of fish are lifted from the oceans of the world every year. When you think of the blessing that God had to pour in to keep that up. And this is a blessed world, and he wants to bless us too, to give us more of the good things that he planted in our lives.

Now let us look at the many objects here. It is not an exhaustive list. There are many things in creation not listed in Genesis 1. God is giving us a list of the things that make up man's environment, the things that we have to deal with – plants and trees and animals, and each other, and the sky and the sea and the land – and so he just keeps it utterly simple. And I want you to notice that the creation did not come instantaneously. It came in stages. That again is a revelation. It is amazing that they knew that right back in the Old Testament days that God did not just say, world, and a second later everything was here. God told us that he made it in stages. And he developed it and science is the first to agree that that is how it happened. So, God took a little time over it. I think he enjoyed making it so much that he wanted to keep doing a bit and then stand back and look at it.

Do you make things that way? Or are you the sort of impatient, panicked person who likes to get it all done in one fell swoop? I am a bit like that I'm afraid. But when I am trying to be patient, I can do a bit and stand back and say, "That's good." Then I do a bit more, stand back and say, "That's even better"; do a bit more and you know, spin it out a bit, and enjoy it. In fact, I seem to remember my parents used to say a lot to me, don't do it all at once. You know, if I was given a jigsaw, I would just head down, and have to be finished. And so, my birthday and Christmas presents would be used up fairly quickly. Don't do it all at once, or don't eat it all at once, you know? And God said, I'm not going to do it all at once, and he didn't do it all at once. He did it in stages.

Now, I would love to spend a lot of time on each day but let us just run quickly through the days and say a few things. The

CREATION

first day – which must have been a very, very long day because it includes the whole period when the earth was in darkness and the period when it was in light – is what made the first evening and the first morning. That is why the Jews count the day from 6pm to 6pm; the evening is the first part of the day. They just copy God that way. It is we who follow the Romans and have it midnight to midnight. But you see, that whole first day was right from verse 1, and through all the darkness and then through the light, and there was evening and morning, the first day. That begins to help us with the problem of the days, actually.

But it all started in darkness. There were two things that were vital for life there. One was matter and the other was water. I wonder if you realise how vital water is to our life? And that this planet is unique for its quantity of water? I am seven-eighths per cent water. I don't have water on the brain I hope, but seven-eighths water! And this applies to almost every living thing. And this unique thing, just two atoms of hydrogen, one of oxygen – and that incredible hydrogen link which means that it will dissolve almost anything – it carries 60 different things around in your blood, things of temperature, and it is the only naturally occurring, inorganic liquid. In theory it should be a gas but it isn't, it is a liquid. And God made water. You know, I could spend the whole of this chapter just discussing water, and you should thank God every time you have a drink. We take it for granted because there is so much around, especially when the heavens open and the lot falls on us. But it is a blessing, I tell you. It is a real blessing.

There was matter, there was water; but one more thing is needed for life – light. And God saw that we got it. We still don't know what light is. We know it travels at an incredibly fast rate – 186,000 miles a second. What a speed! And it has got to come all that way from the sun every morning to reach here, to create light. And it comes. It does not take too long to come. And we still don't know what it is – something to do with electrons moving

Chapter 2: The seven days of creation

from one level of energy to another and causing a flash. We can describe it; we really don't know what it is or how it travels, but we couldn't live without it. God is creating an environment for life, and the care with which he introduces each thing that is absolutely needed. It is crazy to believe this just happened. You are asking me to believe far too much.

When I used to be a chaplain in the Royal Air Force, I was a chaplain to atheists. There were three chaplains – RC, C of E, and OD and I was the OD and that means the Other Denominations or the Odd Bod. And it meant that after the RCs and C of Es had had their pick, I got the rest. So, I got Methodists, Presbyterians, Baptists, Congregationalists, Muslims, Buddhists, Hindus, agnostics, and atheists. And when a man registered as an atheist, the first thing I said to him was, "Congratulations on your faith. I just don't have that much faith. To believe that nothing turned into something and became all this by itself, I just can't believe it, I'm sorry. So let me shake your hand and congratulate you on your faith." The second thing I said to him was, "If you die while you're under my care, I promise you at your funeral there will be no prayers, no hymns, I won't read the Bible, I won't mention God, I'll just say you're dead and gone." And do you know, I found there are many atheists who are prepared to live as atheists; they are not so happy to die as one. And then I generally used to say, "Now sit down and tell me what kind of a god you don't believe in." And you know, when they did, I invariably was able to say, "That makes me an atheist too, because I don't believe in that kind of a god either. You've just been wrongly informed." Oh, how important it is to meet people right where they are. I could not be an atheist. I do not have that much faith, to believe that water – that vital thing to us – that light – that vital thing – that it has all been so perfectly arranged, that within a very narrow tolerance of temperature and distance – we are just the right distance from the sun – that everything is perfectly arranged for life. Don't you ask me to believe that was an

CREATION

accident. I cannot do it – I don't have that much faith. So, Day 1 came and went, and it was a good day.

And Day 2 came and the atmosphere came. Do you know, I would be a dead man if I went 30 miles up or 30 miles down. Those astronauts who went up in the shuttle, they had to take a whole supply of atmosphere with them. When the Russian astronaut came back to earth, they said, "Did you see God?" "Well, no, sorry" – the Russian astronaut came back and said, "I didn't see God and I didn't see any angels." When the American astronaut came back, they said, "Did you see God?" And he said, "No…" They said, "Did you *meet* God?" And he said, "No," but he said, "I would have done if I'd stepped outside my spacesuit." And we are creatures of this little thin atmosphere and we can't go anywhere outside that atmosphere. We will have to take it with us. That is where we belong. And it is good.

Day 3. Here is Genesis telling us that the dry land appeared out of the oceans. How would an ancient Hebrew know that? How would he know that you can climb the Alps and find seashells at the top of them? How would he know that the Basingstoke chalk hills are just made up of millions of tiny sea creatures that lived in the ocean? Again, it has got the stamp of divine revelation on it. What human being would speculate that the highest mountains came up out of the water? And again and again, you will find in Job and the book of Psalms and right the way through how careful God was to decide how far the sea could come and to set its limits. Do you know, if the polar icecaps melted, then the oceans of the world would rise 200 feet and most major cities in the world would be under it, because most major cities are below that 200 feet. And the Thames Barrier would be no use whatsoever. And we sing about it: "Eternal Father strong to save who bids the mighty ocean deep its own appointed limits keep." How precarious we are, but God has said, so far and no farther; that is the limit. And he appointed the dry land and the sea. It has got mind behind it. It is not a mechanism; it is a mind

Chapter 2: The seven days of creation

that thought it all through. And as soon as he got dry land, he said, let's have some vegetation. And at this point I want you to notice that he said, let the *earth* produce vegetation, as if he had somehow built into the soil a capacity to produce plant life.

I want you to notice that little phrase, "Let the *earth produce*", almost as if he said, now you can take over a bit. And that again I think allows some room for natural development within Genesis 1.

Day 4. And I am just rushing through. I will come to the problem later, of the fact that they had light three days before the sun. I will deal with that later. I want you to notice as we go through the positive thing this says: the *sun* is there for me; the moon is there for us – that is an amazing concept; somehow that alters your thinking about the whole universe. You don't feel dwarfed, you don't feel lonely. Do you know, modern man is so frightened of being the only life in the universe that he has got to fill that empty space with science fiction; have you noticed? I find there is a paranoia here with our society. They are saying, "Help, help! Surely there's somebody out there; surely there's life out there; surely there's somebody wanting to visit us." They are. And that is the deep-rooted fear behind all these films. They want to believe somebody is out there. But this is the only planet on which there is this kind of life. But I don't feel frightened by that. I don't feel lonely because of that, because God is out there. And there are angels out there too. There is life out there but it is not the kind of life your science fiction is desperately trying to create. That is just trying to whistle in the dark and I just hope you don't get tied up in all that.

You see, in the ancient world they worshipped the sun. There is even an island in the south seas of the Pacific where they worship the moon, and somebody asked, "Why do you worship the moon?" And they said, "Well, it's more important to us than the sun. The sun comes out during the day when it's light," but they said, "the moon comes out at night when it's dark, so we worship the moon." Isn't it pathetic? But you know, the ancient Egyptians worshipped the sun and this land in which we live worshipped the sun. That is why this day is called *Sun*day. It is not s-o-n, it's s-u-n. And that is why you will celebrate December the 25th, pagan sun festival, it is the birthday of the sun god, when people noticed that the days were getting longer so the sun had been reborn. And we are riddled with sun. And in fact, if a visitor from Mars came here during August, he would assume that 90% of the British people were sun worshippers based on the fact that they would go to the ends of the earth to worship the sun, and prostrate themselves before it. But you see, Genesis says the sun, the moon and the stars are nothing more than God's fairy lights and they are there to serve you. They are there to regulate the earth, they are there to govern the earth so you never get out of balance and he just throws the stars in as a bonus. "And the stars" – as if they are hardly important. And yet the majority of people in your town believe that the stars govern them.

I once had a man say to me, "But surely, it's in the Bible, astrology? Surely there was a star above Bethlehem." I said, "Wrong again." I said, "You're trying to tell me from astrology that the stars in the sky affect a baby's birth on earth." I said, "At Bethlehem, it was the baby's birth on earth that affected the stars. You just got it the wrong way round." And in fact, all those stars and that sun and that moon are there to serve us, that's what God is trying to tell us. He put them there for you. Yes, you can enjoy it. But don't ever be so foolish as to think that you are under them. You are not. They are there to serve you. They are part of God's creation. That should keep you off horoscopes for the rest of your life.

Day 5, aerial and aquatic life. And here, a new word is introduced – *living* creatures, literally moving creatures, literally animated creatures that can decide where they go. Now a plant can't suddenly say, well, I think I'll shift from here. A tree can't say, I'm going down to Bognor Regis for the summer. But there

Chapter 2: The seven days of creation

are tiny birds that travel 6,000 miles for the summer and God says, at this point I had to introduce something fundamentally new. I had to do a creative act again. And so there is a difference between inanimate life and animate life. And the term *living being*, which is applied here, is exactly the same as in Genesis 2, when God breathed into the dust and Adam became an animated being. So, the term *living soul* applies to animals and men in the Bible's terms. It means an animated being, something that decides for itself where it is going. And the animals can do that but the plants cannot and this required a new creative act of God to bring something quite new into the situation, to cause animated creatures to move around the earth. And so, he started with the sea – which science agrees with incidentally – and marine life was born, and the birds came. Later we will see that the animals came too. And he blessed them. I have got a whole lot of figures and numbers. He classifies fish in two groups, the monsters and the tinies. And you know, the biggest creature in the sea is actually 100 thousand million times larger than the smallest creature in the sea. And here is God talking about creating the huge monsters of the deep and the tiny organisms. But that is the difference – a hundred thousand million times, the biggest giant squid compared to the smallest diatom; and God made each of them carefully. If there is one thing that impresses me as I study the universe – and I have sat in an observatory slung under a huge reflector telescope, and I have also spent months in laboratories dissecting things looking through electron microscopes – you find that whether you look through a telescope or a microscope it has all been carefully done. The detail is incredible. He took as much care about the tiny universe of one atom as he did about the entire universe with its whirling bodies in space. And so here are great and small – all creatures great and small – and he had made them both.

Day 6. It is the only day in the Hebrew that is called "*the day*". Up until now it says, "evening and morning, one day", "evening and morning, two days" and then it says, on *the* sixth day – something special is coming up. On *the* sixth day, what is so special? Well, I don't think it is the animals, though they are the nearest form of creature to us, they inhabit the same environment. And once again, men have fallen into idolatry and worshipped animals. You go to India and you look at those sacred cows. It makes you sick. I have been driving through Bombay and seen the little babies lying in the gutter within a foot of the car wheels and nobody seems to mind. And if you run over a baby in the gutter at night, well that's just too bad; that is happening all the time. But if you hit a sacred cow, boy you are in trouble. And that is just crazy. People need liberating by teaching them Genesis 1. Animals are animals and man is man.

Now, I am not going to say anything in this chapter about the creation of man because I want to deal with man as a separate topic in the next chapter; his place in creation; his nature and his environment. I just want you to notice that here he is God's masterpiece, the one part of creation about which God said, let's put ourselves into this. And every artist wants to create a picture that really is him, that really has got all of his creativity in it. You know, if you ask an artist, which is your best picture? He will always say, my next one, because he is striving after the perfect picture that will embody all that he has inside himself. And God said, now we're going to make the masterpiece. And he poured all of himself and so he uses the word *created* three times of this one creature as if there is something so different, so new, so radically different from everything else before, that he just had to do it from scratch.

And it is at that point that we raise a *huge* question about evolution. I can see room in Genesis for evolution within plants, within limits of certain groups of animals, but if you tell me that I came out of a zoo or that I crawled out of a slime, you destroy me; you treat me as an animal – and I am not! And God wanted to say that so he said three times: created, created, created.

Chapter 2: The seven days of creation

And because this touched his heart more than any other part of creation, he put it in poetry. And in my paraphrase, I tried to give you a little rhyme in there to get that across to you.

Day 7. Day off. Great. I want to say something about this day off. To me it is vital and, incidentally, it is a long day because it didn't end for thousands and thousands of years. So, the first day was a very long one and the last day was a very long one, which means that the ones in between are likely to be rather long as well. But I am coming back to that. It never says there was evening and morning on the seventh day because God was still in it when this was written. And he completed his work of creation. The idea that God has gone on creating is not true. Everything he wanted to make has been made. Now he keeps it all going, yes, and he supplies its need, yes. And it is interesting that both laws of thermodynamics confirm this. Now you see that is the kind of scientific jargon we can drop in.

Let me try to explain it and communicate it simply. There are certain things that scientists have discovered about our universe which seem to apply everywhere and all the time that seem as near fixed ideas as you can get. And in particular there are two laws they have discovered concerning energy which seem so fixed that you could bet your last pound on them. And they call them the laws of thermodynamics, which is a big word for energy. And the first law of thermodynamics is that the amount of energy in this universe is constant; it stays exactly the same. It may change its form from one form to another but it is the same. Now it can't always have been like that. There must have been a point when the energy was put into the system. It is as if they are saying the car as it is running now has exactly the same amount of petrol in it the whole way. Actually, your car does in a sense. The petrol changes into other forms but the energy level stays the same. You have used some of it to push you along but there is still the same amount of energy but now a lot of it has been lost to the atmosphere. But the energy is still there.

CREATION

Now, if that is so, then energy must have always existed. There must have been a period when the energy was being put into the system and then it must have stopped needing to be put in and it just kept going, do you follow me? So that seems to point to a completion of the winding up process of putting the petrol into the tank.

But the second law of thermodynamics also points in the same way. And that law is this: It is the law of entropy, which means that in practical terms, energy is for practical purposes running down, because it is becoming less and less available. As we change energy from one form into another it is more difficult to get hold of it again. Once you have burned the energy in your petrol tank or the coal in your stove, or whatever energy you use to heat your house, it is terribly difficult to get hold of it again, isn't it? It is terribly difficult keeping it in. You insulate your house but it tends to get beyond your reach, so that for practical purposes, even though the level of energy does stay the same in this universe, it is getting more and more locked up in a form that we can't handle and can't reach, so it is virtually running down. The oil reserves that I saw from the air – I looked down on the oil rigs in the North Sea and I thought, oil will run out and we won't be able to get hold of the energy again.

Therefore, in practical terms, we are in a universe that is running down. There must have been a time when it was wound up, because you cannot have a universe that is forever running down. How did it start? And so, on the seventh Day God said, right, I've finished what I'm putting in to this. Do you follow me now? I've put all the energy into it, I've put all the matter into it, I've put all the forms of life into it that I'm going to. And he completed his work, and the Bible does not teach continuous creation. And God said, now I'm going to have a day off, a day to myself. And ever since he has said, and you need a day for me too. And just as I'm a God who doesn't get totally wrapped up in my work, you mustn't either because I've made you in my

Chapter 2: The seven days of creation

image, so you see that you get a day off. Wasn't that beautiful of God to think of that?

And you know, all the other divisions of time in our world are related to the sun or the moon or some natural process. There is only one period of time that is not related to anything natural and it is the week, and you got that from God. So, if you enjoy your weekend you should say, thank you Lord; I wouldn't have had that but for you. The Roman Empire did not have a week. They did not have a weekly break like we do. They had a month-end not a weekend. And you will find that people have tried to destroy the week. In the French Revolution they decided to destroy the Christian week and so they went in for an eight-day week and it wasn't long before they were in trouble.

The same happened in World War I. We need a weekly break. But the animals don't need it. The ducks in my back garden don't have a weekly break. I don't see them saying, hey, it's Sunday, you know? It is not natural. Now it is natural to go by the sun and by the moon, it is natural to have years and months, but it is not natural to have weeks. And I tell you, in a godless society it won't be long before you lose your weekends. Sunday trading has come back, and it is yet another straw on the water that we are getting away from Genesis 1 and losing our humanity, which is a reflection of deity.

I am trying to help you see how practical Genesis 1 is. It is related to having a weekend, it is related to reading your horoscope, it is related to all these things. It gives us our place in the world.

Now I would like to tackle the problems a bit now. I want to tackle those three problems. I would like to deal with the three major issues between science and Scripture and just give you guidelines about how to approach them rather than a complete answer because we haven't time for that.

In theory, science and Scripture should never contradict each other. If science stuck to discussing how things came to be and

CREATION

Scripture stuck to why they came to be and who brought them into being, they would not overlap at all, but fortunately or unfortunately, Genesis 1 also ventures across the border into how at certain points. And within the overlap, science studying how and Genesis studying why, when they get into each other's territory and there is an overlap, then there are real points of friction. And there are three questions that science has raised about Genesis 1, from its examination of the evidence in the world.

The first is the sequence in which things appeared – the order. The second is the speed with which they came. And the third is the principle of selection that left us with what we have got. Now, I hope you can recall my parable of the invisible snooker player and my attempt to try and show you that there are certain battles over fact, but there is a war on over faith, and we are going to be touching that distinction right now.

So, let us look at sequence. I begin by pointing out that there is a remarkable correspondence between science and Scripture. There is more in common with the order than the differences. Science agrees that matter came before life and that the sea came before the land, and that the animals came before man. There is a whole correspondence. In general terms, Genesis 1 is the same order as science has discovered but there are two sorts of exception. One is an astronomical one and the other is a biological one. The astronomical one is the huge problem that light came on Day 1 and the sun and moon came in Day 4.

Now, all sorts of explanations have been given, that there must have been some bright star or that there were some other nebulae or some other source of light and so on. I have looked as carefully as I can at this and I have come to the conclusion that it is an example of what I told you at the beginning of this chapter, of God looking at it from our point of view. And there are scientific indications as well as in Genesis that the first three days the earth was covered with mist, with a thick shroud and that the light that got through was only diffused light; that there

Chapter 2: The seven days of creation

had to be a major change in the composition of the atmosphere before the sky could go clear. In particular, a reduction in carbon dioxide, which would be brought about when the plants started to develop.

They would have enough diffused light to develop but they would then start breathing in the carbon dioxide and breathing out oxygen and clearing the atmosphere. You know that if you plant forests, you change the sky; you change the microclimate when you plant a lot of trees. And therefore, from the perspective of a man standing on the earth and looking up, the sun, moon and stars would not be in the sky until that clearing had happened and therefore, he would be aware of light generally – vague, diffused – but in that fourth phase he could have looked up and seen, oh, my, there's a sun and moon and the stars there. In other words, it is what is called phenomenal language, which means describing a thing as it *appears* and therefore, if you like, I am prepared to say that I believe – and I do – that the sun, moon and stars *appeared* and were appointed to do their job on that fourth day in God's sight.

That is my own understanding because of the whole earth-centred upward look in Genesis 1. Now, that may not satisfy you but I just give that to you for what it is worth. There are one or two other possible explanations but they seem to me not really to fit the bill, and to raise more problems than they resolve.

The biological ones I am going to say a little more about – plants before marine life, fruit trees before fishes, birds before insects, whales before reptiles, birds before reptiles and man before woman. Here are biological difficulties in which things in Genesis 1 do not seem to be in the right order and where there are *minor discrepancies*, you may say, not major ones. I have come to the conclusion that the order in Genesis 1 is only partly chronological and is primarily logical.

If I were trying to describe to a child very, very simply how a house got built I would tend to say that the first chap who came was the bricklayer and the second chap who came was the carpenter and then came the plumber and then came the electrician and then came the plasterer and then came the decorator and then they all went on their holidays. And in just seven simple steps I would describe for a child to grasp the different things that were needed *and* in the order in which they were needed. But my hobby is architecture and I have been involved in quite a few buildings and in bar charts or critical path analyses. I am so glad that God didn't think, I'll have to give them a critical path analysis in Genesis 1 – but if he had, then you would have to work out the kind of bar, in which things can overlap and they don't always begin and end just like that.

And the fact that the holidays began for some a little earlier than the others does not alter the fact that, in simple terms, the central part of each activity followed a progressive order. Now you can either tell somebody in a very complicated way through a critical path analysis exactly when a certain trade started or if you are just wanting to get across the truth that certain different trades were needed, and in an order, then you do what you do with a child and you are giving the child a story of how the house was built that is part chronological and part logical or topical if you follow me. And I believe all these little differences that scientists have pointed out are due to the fact that God chose to give us a simple story rather than a critical path analysis. And you are asking too much of Genesis 1 if you want to get every little detail of chronology tied up. God is concerned to give you the basic story. Do you follow me?

Now again, that may solve the problem for you or it may not, but it does for me. And I just say, Lord, I thank you that you are an architect but that you didn't give me a critical path analysis. It would have taken half the Bible.

Now, the second question that I want to deal with is this matter of the *days*, the speed. It is a most familiar clash. Scripture says six days, science says four billion years for our earth and as I

Chapter 2: The seven days of creation

said, there is a slight difference there that we have got to face. This has not been helped by scholars of the Bible trying to work out the date of creation, and people have. If you have an old Authorised Version, you probably have seen the date 4004 BC above Genesis 1. Anyway, in the old Bibles they have 4004. That was worked out by Archbishop Ussher of Ireland who tried to work back through all the generations, and came to the conclusion that it was about 4004 BC that creation happened, so he wrote it in the Bible. I wish he hadn't.

God did not put a date in. There is not a date in Genesis until chapter 5. So, if God did not put dates in, then we should not either. But he did, and then along came a Cambridge scholar called Lightfoot and he worked it out even more carefully and he actually put in his Bible that it took place between 18 October and the 24th in the year 4004 BC with Adam being created at 9 o'clock in the morning on October the 23rd. And somebody dryly said, "Being a careful scholar, he didn't want to commit himself more fully than that." Now frankly, people who start putting dates and times like that in, they have just made it even worse for us and brought the whole thing into disrepute. If God didn't date creation, then don't you either. God didn't *tell* you when he created the heavens and the earth. There is no date on it at all, so we don't need to fall into that trap. But he did say six days.

There are five possible ways of interpreting the days of Genesis, and I give you all five and leave you to make your own judgement on this. But you see, I believe that two things can happen when science and Scripture disagree. Either the scientist has got his interpretation of the facts wrong or the Christian has got his interpretation of the Scripture wrong. And it is very important to find out which it is. It could even be both. So, are we sure that we are right in saying the day in Genesis 1 is a 24-hour period? Well, certainly the word *Yom*, which is Hebrew for *day*, is largely used for a period of 24 hours in the Bible. Twelve hundred times it is used for a period of 24 hours. So, people

CREATION

assume, then, that it must mean that in Genesis 1 and the phrase *morning and evening* seems to convince them totally that it does.

The problem if you believe in six literal days is that you have got to find some time somewhere for the geological data that we now know we have got. Now, where do you find that time? And there are three ways people have tried to find it. One is the *Gap Theory*, in which they say, in Genesis 1, verse 2 there is a huge amount of time and they translate it, "And the earth *became* formless and void," and say that creation went wrong in that verse, and for ages it lay in that bad state and that is where geology comes in. Now I cannot accept that because it means that the whole of Genesis 1 is a reconstruction job and not a creation job and I just can't go along with it. And it twists the language.

A second way you find some time for geology is the *Flood*, and there is a spate of books coming out now sparked off by a couple of men called Whitcomb and Morris who try and squeeze all the geological data into the twelve months of Noah's Flood. And I am sorry, but it just won't go. It is a quart into a pint pot.

The third way is what is called the *Antique Theory*, which says that God produced genuine fraudulent antiques, and it asks, if God made a tree, how many rings did he put in the trunk the day he made it? So that if you cut it down the next day, you would say, that tree's thirty years old, but it wasn't. It was a genuine fraudulent antique. Do you follow me? And that God deliberately made the rocks look old so that they looked like an antique to us, but they are not actually that old. Now, I am sorry, but my Father does not play tricks with my mind. He is not that kind of a God, and he does not tease us. So, I am sorry but that will not do, and frankly I cannot interpret the days of Genesis 1 literally.

I have already indicated that Day 1 was much longer than 24 hours, and Day 7 certainly was. Shall I tell you when Day 7 ended? It ended on the first Easter Sunday and that is when God started creating again. And he is into the new creation now. But from Genesis 1 through to the first Easter Sunday, God was

Chapter 2: The seven days of creation

having a rest from creation. Now he is creating again; this time around, he has started with people and he is finishing with the world. He is doing it the other way round this time, but the new creation began with the resurrection of Jesus from the dead. He is the firstborn of the new universe that is coming, and his resurrection body is the first man to be made for the new universe.

So, Day 1 was long, Day 7 was long, so I am afraid I think the others were long too. Does that mean that the second interpretation is right, that each day is a geological day? And the Hebrew word *Yom* can mean a long period. Sixty-five times in the Old Testament it means a very long period. In Genesis chapter 2 it says, "In the *day* when God made heaven and earth and all that is in them". And that was at least seven days or even longer.

So, is it the simplest way just to say Day 1 was a very long time and Day 2 was a very long time and Day 3 was a very long time? No, I don't think that will do because it doesn't do justice to "morning and evening". For some reason God told us it was in days not ages and I have got to ask, Lord, what were you saying?

The third possible interpretation is this. These days are mythological, they are part of the fable, they are a fairy story, they are pretend days and they are just part of the framework of the story and they have no significance at all. That is the favourite modern liberal view. It is a myth, it is a fairy tale, it is what the BBC calls *faction*, it is a mixture of fact and fiction. And the days are part of the fiction and what happened in them is the fact. Now, I don't feel that God is going to give us faction, do you? It is a most dangerous thing, is faction, because you can pick and choose what you believe is fact. So I cannot go along with the mythological.

The fourth intriguing one, which some evangelical scholars have tried, is the educational one. These are school days, and what I mean by that is that Moses went to school for seven days and on the first day, God taught him about light and darkness, on the second day God taught him about sea and sky – you have got

CREATION

the picture. Professor Wiseman of London University is perhaps the best-known man who has propounded that one in his book, which is appropriately called *Creation Revealed in Six Days*. But I am sorry, it won't wash with me. That is again having to twist God's words.

I am left with the fact that God wanted to tell me that he created the world in six days, and so I am left with a final interpretation and you will get to know me, but I usually give you all the interpretations and the one that appeals to me last. But this last one is to me the right one. It fits all the facts and it is that these days are to be interpreted theologically – they are God days. God knew perfectly well we would find out that the earth took four billion years. He must have known that, so why did he still say six days? Because time is relative; and to God, it was less than a week's work. And to him, it was a week and at this point he is saying, to me, if you want to get my feel of this, it was all in a week's work.

You see, we are saying that to God time is relative and "a thousand years is as a day and a day is as a thousand years". And you will find that the time scale throughout the Bible is he rushes through all the geological ages in just a week and then you will find that time slows down. We rush through the centuries in the Old Testament; we get into the New Testament, then we rush through three years. And it is slowing down, and it slows down until you are looking at days, and in the last week in the life of the Lord, every day is mentioned. And then the last day, it is every hour, until Jesus died; you go through the third hour, the sixth hour, the ninth hour. And what the Bible is saying is, the longest day God ever had was the day his Son died. Do you follow me? Creation was just... You see? You get God's perspective because if you go by science, you will lose all significance. I can prove that.

Imagine Cleopatra's Needle is standing in front of you, the one on Thames Embankment, the one that Moses used to look

Chapter 2: The seven days of creation

at every day he went to school by the way. Cleopatra's Needle, it was; it was one of two at the entrance to the university in Egypt. Imagine Cleopatra's Needle. If that represents the age of our earth, a penny flat on top of it would represent the time man has been on the earth and a postage stamp on top of that – its thickness would represent the recorded history of man as it is not like that at all. To me, the relativity of time meant that all the work of creation was a week. To me, it was just six days and then a day off. The important part of time to me is what happens now on the earth. Do you follow me? It is a God dimension of time. These are God days. And if you think of God doing a week's work, then you won't get overwhelmed with all those billions of years that science talks about. You won't feel a nobody. You will realise that now is the day that is important to God.

Now, I believe that does justice to the language and it puts us in our proper place and it is just saying that God is on flexitime. And that he is talking about *his* days and he wants us to go on thinking of creation in the week and then we will keep it in perspective and we won't get overwhelmed. Because that is what it was to him, and when he made you, he says, and you'd better operate on the same principle, do your week's work and have a day off. Mind you, I have yet to hear a preacher preach on the text, "Six days shalt thou labour". Do you know what I mean? It is a five-day week now.

But do you remember Jacob? It says, Jacob served seven years for Rachel and it seemed but a few days for love of Rachel. Now, that, I believe, is what is being said here. To God, it seemed a few days to get the whole thing made and to get it all filled with creatures, and now he is getting on with the important bit. And the longest day to God was the day that his Son died. Every hour seemed an eternity and we need to get God's feel of time and then we will get creation and history in balance. Otherwise, you lose it.

I am going to stop there because the third issue is a pretty big

CREATION

one. That is the selection, whether it was natural or supernatural and Darwin and all that. And we are going to have to look at that in detail. So let me sum up.

The message of Genesis 1 about our world is just this. It is an orderly world because it was an ordered world. Nothing happened that God did not bring about. If he had not been involved at every stage, nature of herself would have produced nothing and in fact, I will tell you a secret: the Bible has no word for *nature*. It is only those who don't want to believe in God who use the term nature. It is those who don't want God as their Father who talk about Mother Nature producing us. Have you noticed that? And it is idolatry – it is turning nature into a god and saying nature did this, nature produced the monkeys, nature produced man, as if nature was somehow a person even, or at best, a power that could do it. And Genesis 1 said nothing would have happened. Sometimes God changed what was already there into something else. Sometimes he did something quite new and next time I am going to show you that the fossil record, the evidence all points to Genesis 1 and not to Darwin. The evidence is there for all to see, the results of what Genesis 1 says God did. And it does not fit in with natural selection. It fits in with supernatural.

What is at stake in all this? Very simply this – if the evidence, as I shall show you, points to creation rather than evolution, points to supernatural production rather than natural process, points to a personal choice for all of us being here rather than an impersonal chance, points to a world in which we may exercise faith, hope and love rather than fatalism, helplessness and luck, a world in which we can believe in Providence rather than coincidence. A world in which God is Lord rather than man is lord, then what is at stake in all this? I will tell you this. Why is there so much prejudice against creation? Very simple – people do not want to live in an ordered world because they do not want to be ordered. It is as simple as that. And we will find that

Chapter 2: The seven days of creation

Genesis 3 explains how we got in a condition where we wanted to be God and we said, "No Lord, we're not having you ordering us around; we don't like an ordered universe. We'll admit it's orderly but we don't want it ordered. No, thank you." And that is the root of it and Genesis 1 is going to challenge us deeply.

Do you want to live an ordered life? Or would you prefer to believe in luck? After all, if you live in an ordered life, then you have responsibilities but if you live in a disordered world, then you only have rights. And those who prefer to talk about rights rather than responsibilities will always prefer evolution to creation. They will always prefer a chance world to a chosen world. They will always prefer to regard themselves as an accident rather than the design of a loving Creator.

CHAPTER 3:

THE ORIGIN OF MAN

It was on the first day of the week that God said, "Let there be light" and began the work of the old creation. It was on the first day of the week that he began his work of new creation and in fact, it was on this day that Jesus rose from the dead and his physical body was the first part of the new creation to be made. And it was on this day that the Holy Spirit was sent down. It is an exciting day because Sunday is the first day of the new creation. That is not my theme for this chapter.

Now, I have decided not to press on with the question of evolution but to go straight into a study of the creation of man. In the first chapter we looked at God. In the second chapter we looked at the world but in this chapter I felt we should consider man. And then, having seen all that the Bible says, we can look at some of the problems that science is raising. But I just got a sense that God does not want science to set the agenda. He wants Scripture to set the agenda and then we can face the problems that science raises. So, I felt we should press on in this chapter and look at man and his origin, his nature, his relationships that are written down for us in Genesis, the end of chapter 1 and the whole of chapter 2. So let me start reading at verse 26 of chapter 1, and again I shall read a paraphrase just to make it fresh.

"At this point God reached a momentous decision. 'Now let us make some different creatures, more our kind, human beings just like us. They can be in charge of all the others, the fish in the sea, the birds of the air and the animals on the land.' To resemble himself God created mankind to reflect in themselves his heart,

CREATION

will and mind, to relate to each other, male and female entwined. Then he affirmed their unique position with words of generous encouragement: 'Produce many offspring for you are to occupy and control the whole earth. The fish in the sea, the birds of the air and the animals on the land are all yours to master. I am also giving you seed-bearing plants and fruit-bearing trees as your food supply. The birds and the beasts can have the green leaves for their food.' And so it was. God surveyed everything he had made and he was very satisfied. It was all so right, so beautiful. Outer space and planet Earth were now complete in all their vastness and variety. Since nothing more was needed God took a break the next day. This is why he designated each seventh day as a special day set apart from the others as a day for himself alone because on that day he was not busy with what had been his daily work.

"This is how our universe was born and how everything in it came to be the way it is. During the time the God Who Is was producing outer space and planet Earth, there was a time when there was no vegetation at all on the ground and if there had been there was neither any rain to irrigate it nor any man to cultivate it. But underground water welled up to the surface and watered the soil and the God Who Is moulded a human body from tiny particles of clay, gave it the kiss of life and man joined the living creatures. Now the God Who Is had already laid out a stretch of parkland east of here in a place called Eden, which means delight, and he brought the first man there to live. The God Who Is had planted a great variety of trees in the park with beautiful foliage and delicious fruit.

"Right in the middle were two rather special trees. The fruit of one could maintain life indefinitely while the fruit of the other gave the eater personal experience of right and wrong. One river watered the whole area but divided into four watercourses as it left the park. One was called the Pishon and wound across the entire length of Havilah, the land where pure nuggets of gold

Chapter 3: The origin of man

were later found as well as aromatic resin and onyx. The second was called the Gihon and meandered right through the country of Cush. The third is the present Tigris, which flows in front of the city of Ashur and the fourth is the present Euphrates.

"So the God Who Is put this man in the parkland of delight to develop and protect it. And the God Who Is gave him very clear orders: 'You are perfectly free to eat the fruit of any tree except one, the tree that brings experience of right and wrong. If you taste that you will have to be put to death.' Then the God Who Is thought aloud, 'it isn't right for the man to be all on his own. I will provide him with a matching partner.' Now the God Who Is had fashioned all sorts of birds and beasts out of the soil and he brought them in contact with the man to see how he would describe them and whatever the man said about each one became its name so the man labelled all the other creatures. But in none of them did he see a real companion for himself.

"So the God Who Is sent the man into a deep coma and while he was unconscious he took tissue from the side of his body and pulled the flesh together over the gap. Then with the tissue he produced a female clone and introduced her to the man and Adam burst out, 'At last you have granted my wish, a companion with my bones and flesh; woman to me is her name; by coming from man, she's the same.' That explains why a man lets go of his parents and holds on to his wife, their two bodies fusing into one again. The first man and his new wife wandered about the park quite bare without the slightest embarrassment."

Right, well I hope that brought it freshly to you. It was one of the world's leading evolutionists, a man called Eton, who said that man must be one of the most improbable productions of the universe. And those who believe that we are simply an accident, a biological mistake, are the first to say that if man had not appeared once, then it is almost certain he would never have appeared again, such are the statistical chances against someone like me appearing on planet Earth. That is what the evolutionists say.

CREATION

But am I a mistake? Am I a cosmic orphan? Am I someone who was not wanted and simply happened? Is it pure chance that man appeared on this planet Earth? If that is so, then, frankly, life is absurd; it is meaningless; it is a sick joke. And that is where we are left if I am an accident and the result of chance rather than choice. It would mean that when I got to the end of my life I would say, "I have missed the point," and then I would ask, "But was there any point to miss?" And I can think of nothing more devastating to a human being than to tell them they were not wanted; they are an accident and there is no point in them being here. It is quite devastating – which means that there are many people alive today who are suffering what is called a crisis of identity.

I remember a man who rang me up at 3 o'clock in the morning. He'd had a drink or two first and he would always "prime the pump" before he ever rang me up and so the telephone used to go at very ungodly hours and at 3 o'clock in the morning I am not a very good Christian. But I remember him ringing up and saying, "Who am I? Who am I?" And this is *the* fundamental question. I guess most of us go through a teenage crisis of identity when we look in the mirror and think, who am I? When you first begin to shave or when you grow up a bit and you think, "Who am I really?" And you go through that crisis; everybody does in their teens. But the vast majority of adults never get through that crisis and they still do not know who they are.

Where do we fit in? If there is a script, what role do I play, or is life simply a journey from nowhere to nowhere? Now, the two brothers Johnny and Desmond Morris have done all they can to persuade me that I am an animal. Johnny Morris does it by looking at animals and seeing human beings, and his brother Desmond does it by looking at human beings and seeing animals and calling us naked apes. But those two brothers between them have conveyed to me that I am just an animal, and if that is all you can say about me, you must not blame me for behaving as if I am in a jungle.

Chapter 3: The origin of man

It is certainly true that functionally I can be classified with animals. Functionally, I am a mammal. Functionally, I inhabit the same environment as the animals. And indeed, Genesis puts my creation in the same day as the animals. And there are many similarities. Yet there are two things that puzzle me if I am nothing more than an animal. And both concern the fact that I do not really feel at home in this world, nor does any person. The animals do, but I don't. And I have yet to meet a human being who felt totally at home in this world. Yet the animals obviously do.

And the two things that worry me about being told I am an animal are these. Number one, I can rise far above the animals, and number two, I can fall way below them. I can act a good deal better than they can and a good deal worse. And the range of my experience is far wider than the animals, far above them and far below them. Far above them, I could list a whole host of things but they are so obvious you hardly need me to tell you. In language, in arts, in culture, in just asking questions. I don't know an animal that asks a question. And my ability to ask questions means that I can think about this world. No animal does. No animal knows what this world once was and no animal can think about what it will yet be. There is a whole range of mental activity, there is a whole range of emotional life, there is a whole range of moral experience.

So far as I know, there is no such thing as a good dog. I have heard them often called that when they have been taught a Pavlovian reaction to beg for food, but a dog has never thought in terms of being good and has never felt any shame at being bad, just fear of punishment. So, there is no such thing as a good dog. Indeed, Jesus said there is no such thing as a good man. "Don't call anyone good but God only" – which is quite a sobering thought. And we use the phrase so glibly that we talk about a good meal. But there is a whole range of moral experience which no animal has.

CREATION

There is a range of spiritual experience which no animal has. I have not yet seen an animal put its paws together and pray. There is no trace of spiritual or religious activity in the whole animal world – not anywhere. So that in all these areas, man can rise so far above the animals that it raises the question as to whether he is one.

But then the opposite is also true and this is shattering – that men can sink way below the animals. I pick out just two areas: sex and violence. I have yet to meet an animal who engages in kinky sex. And I have yet to meet a species that has an Auschwitz for another species. And in these areas alone, and there are others I could list, man falls far below the animals. And we talk about man behaving in a bestial fashion or a beastly fashion. I think that is an insult to the beasts because the hairy apes do not behave as badly as the naked ones.

Now, in these two things, not only in our ability to rise above animals but our ability to fall way below them, there is something unique about man which separates him radically in a difference of kind and not just degree from the animals. And this wide spectrum of experience leaves us floundering around not really knowing where we belong. We swing from the sensual to the spiritual. We swing from materialism to high moral aspiration. In every one of us there is a desire to be a saint and an enjoyment of being a sinner. And we flounder around in this world. We want a heaven and since this earth is not very heavenly, we are constantly looking for some other place that would be heaven to live. And yet, earth is our home.

And man becomes a riddle. I came across a verse of a poem by Alexander Pope which sums it up superbly. He wrote, "Created half to rise, and half to fall; / Great lord of all things, yet a prey to all; / Sole judge of truth, in endless errors hurl'd: / The glory, jest, and riddle of the world!" That just about sums me up. "The glory, jest, and riddle of the world," a completely crazy mixed-up kid. The boy who went to school with a new jersey, BAIK

Chapter 3: The origin of man

embroidered on it, was asked, "What does that mean?" And he said, "Boy, Am I Confused." And they said, "You don't spell confused with a K, you spell it with a C." And he said, "Boy, you don't know how confused I am." And H. G. Wells wrote about a character called Mr Polly and he says of Mr Polly that "he was not so much a human being as a civil war," and this just describes the sentence of Saint Paul, "For the good that I would I do not: but the evil which I would not, that I do." It just sums up this floundering being called man who wonders where he fits in, and has often come to the conclusion that in fact he is a misfit. Now all that summary I have given you so far, you could glean from humanist literature, from the arts, from novels. But you won't get it in the Bible.

What you get in the Bible is an explanation about this strange being that I am. I am not a misfit but I am a hybrid. I am a crossbred person. I belong to two worlds, not one. And I will never really feel at home until those two have become one. I belong to heaven and to earth, which is why my future destiny is not in heaven – and that is naïve Christian teaching. My future destiny is in a new heaven and a new earth. And I don't know when I last heard a sermon on the new earth. I have heard plenty on heaven but none on the new earth. But it is precisely because I am a creature of two worlds that I need to live in a new heaven and a new earth. And my constant inconsistency and contradiction and wavering from one world to the other is due to the fact that I am a hybrid. I have come from two places. I have come from a subhuman and a superhuman source. And that is why I feel trapped in this world. This world is not my home and yet it has to be.

Well now, that is an introduction to what the Bible says about the beginnings of man because as with Alex Haley, as I mentioned in the first chapter, to go back to your roots is to discover who you are. Because Alex Haley found himself living outwardly the life of a white American but inwardly living a life of a black

African and he could not figure it out. There were two kinds of worlds in his heart tugging him and he had to go back to Africa to find his origins to understand why he felt as he did. And we are going to go back to our origins.

Now, first we go back to see what Genesis 1 says about man, and then we will look more fully at Genesis 2. Genesis 1 says a bit. At first sight, it looks as if it is saying we are part of the animal kingdom, created on the sixth day with the rest of the animals to inhabit the same environment. But in fact, Genesis 1 puts the emphasis on the difference between animals and man. And there are 10 differences listed in Genesis 1 between animals and man. Some of them are a bit subtle, others are very obvious.

The first one is fairly subtle and may not come out in an English translation. And it is this, that all the way through Genesis 1 in the Hebrew it says, Day 1, Day 2, Day 3, Day 4, Day 5, and then it says, "on *the* sixth day". It singles out that day as the most important of all six, as if something happened on that day that put all the others into the shade.

The second thing that indicates a difference is that man is the last creative act. With man, creation is over, it is finished. There is no higher creation. He is the grand finale. He is the climax. And it is interesting that science agrees with Scripture here that man was the final creative thing to appear.

The third difference is that with the animals, God simply made a decision and issued an order and said, "Let there be..." but with man, God held a conference first and for the first time the word "us" appears. And it is certainly not the royal we. I have read commentators who say, "Oh well, the plural here is just the royal we, you know, like the queen saying, 'We are going to Balmoral.'" But do you remember I told you that the verbs are singular? Can you imagine Her Majesty the Queen saying, "We am going to Windsor?" If you are going to be royal, you are consistent with it. And yet all the way through Genesis, it is we am, and I explained that to you, that it is the first hint that

Chapter 3: The origin of man

God is a family, not just one Person, and the word that is used is plural, not dual for two but plural for three. And so, he calls the other two in and he says, now let's have a little conference. Let's do something altogether. Whereas before, as I told you, he has been simply issuing "orders" to the Holy Spirit, who was hovering over the chaos and who was carrying out what Father said, Now he calls them together and he says, let's make something special just like us.

Can you sense that God is just catching his breath a bit? Did you get that feel? That God is sort of pausing before this last one? As if there is something terribly important going to happen. Come together, now let's... Do you get that sense? I may be reading too much into this but I just get the sense that God was realising the risk he was taking with this last step. It was going to be the crown of creation but it could be the crucifixion of it at the same time. He was going to create a being capable of being a companion to him, capable of having relationships with him but also capable of rebellion; capable of messing the whole thing up. If he had stopped with the animals, the creation would have perfectly obeyed his will forever.

I almost get the feeling of a bachelor who has got a lovely house and dogs and a budgerigar and a beautiful garden full of flowers and is very happy with it all, and he is wondering whether to get married, wondering whether having a wife will spoil the whole thing. Do you know what I mean? Because he is realising that another person in that situation, with a will of their own, is going to be very different from a nice garden and the pets and a beautiful house. I just get that sense, that God is just pausing and saying, it's a big step this; something terribly important is going to happen. It could ruin the whole thing. I just sense a kind of pause and a bated breath. But it makes man quite different from the animals, this "Let us..."

The fourth thing is that the word "created" not only is used for the third time only in Chapter 1, but is used three times for this one creature. Now that had never happened before. As if God is emphasising three times that this is a new departure that would not have happened if he had not decided. So, the idea that man naturally descended from animals is just contrary to scriptural teaching. Man would not have appeared unless God had decided that something quite different was to be brought into being. And I think the evolutionist is just plain blind when he can make the statement that he does make that man is the most Improbable creature to have appeared, and not realised that it was the result of a deliberate decision. On his own premises it is so unlikely that a man would have appeared. So God said, "Let's do it." It all makes sense. I will show you next time that the fossil record is far more consistent with creation than with what is popularly called evolution.

The next thing, difference number 5. God bursts into poetry. Now, you only do that when your heart is being touched. Prose is for the head; poetry is for the heart. And when love comes into the picture, you invariably start writing poetry. And all the way up until now, God has simply described in prose – I said this and it happened; and I did that and it happened; and now suddenly he is into poetry. He does not write poetry about the plants; he does not write poetry about the animals. He is not a William Wordsworth. But he writes poetry about man as if he is saying, this is touching my heart.

Difference number 6 is the most obvious one. He says, man will be in our image, our likeness. Now I have seen so much ink spilled about which part of man is like God. Well, let us just look at some of the answers. People usually say, well of course our bodies are not like God because God is Spirit and doesn't have a body. I am not sure that that is valid thinking. It is right that God does not have a body; it is wrong to say that my body is not like him because everything I can do with my body, he can do without one. And that is why there is no problem in the Bible about talking about the eyes of God, the ears of God, the

Chapter 3: The origin of man

nostrils of God, the mouth of God, the hand of God, the arm of God, the kidneys of God, the heart of God, the feet of God. You will find that my whole body corresponds in some way to the functions God fulfils without a body. So, I am not prepared to rule out my body as being in the likeness of God otherwise you are left with an impossible Bible that is full of references to such things.

Now, God does not have a body but what I am saying is everything my hand can do he can do without a hand so that I can look at my hand and think about the hand of God and it does not distort my understanding. Mentally, I am intelligent. I don't know what my quotient is but I can think, I can reflect, I have an appreciation of truth. And God is like that too. And then aesthetically, I have an appreciation of beauty; so does God. Morally I am aware of the fact that there is a difference between right and wrong even if my conscience has been conditioned by my upbringing. I know there are lines to be drawn and that is something I got from God.

I could go on and make a whole long list of the different things in me that are like God but I just want to say it is the whole thing that is like God, not parts. I think we make a big mistake if we say, which part of you is like God? The whole of you is like God. It is all these things put together and just to try to find a bit of God in someone is, I think, to approach it wrongly. He made *man* in his image, not a bit of man but the whole being is like God. Which means that God is like man and that is revolutionary. That is why it is so foolish to make a golden calf and say that is God. You have moved much further away from God if you look at an animal. It is man who is like God. And you should be able to look at everybody in the tube train or the bus and say, God's like that person sitting over there. You should see his image there however distorted, however covered up. There is an image of God which the Bible teaches no man loses. It is interesting that the image is not such a spiritual thing that only believers have it. Unbelievers, wicked sinners, are said in the Bible still to be in the image of God and to have his likeness in them. And that gives every human being a dignity; that is what stops euthanasia, that is what stops abortion, that is what stops killing off the mentally retarded – because there is an image, a resemblance, there. And it is one truth that we really need to recover in our society. When you lose that truth, you finish up with inhumanity and injustice but it is the whole that is in the image.

The next thing I want to say is not only is God like us but it means that a human being is capable of containing the Godhead. Now think of that. You see, if this is not true – what is said in Genesis 1 – then it is not true that the fullness of the Godhead dwelt in Jesus bodily. But you see, Charles Wesley in his hymns says it in an amazing way: "Our God contracted to a span incomprehensibly made man." And the fullness of the Godhead got into a human body under six feet tall in Jesus. There is an incredible connection in here that we need to almost take our shoes off for and wonder at. I am like God; therefore, God is like me; therefore, it is possible for God to be a human being and the Incarnation is possible because men were made in the image of God.

The seventh difference is in male and female. Now, astonishingly, Genesis 1 says that the male and female character of mankind links us with God rather than the animals. Most people make the very fundamental mistake of thinking that is something we got from animals. But Genesis 1 says, "In the image of God created he them, male and female he created them." In other words, God could not put his image into just one person. Now think of that. He had to create complementary natures. Now to me it is an amazing thing about Jesus that he was never married but I have yet to meet a woman who does not feel that Jesus understands her perfectly.

But the normal human life is this: Since God is not one person all on his own but three in perfect oneness, he decided to just

Chapter 3: The origin of man

reduce that by one and make mankind two in oneness. So that we might understand that no one person is complete. God is a society; mankind is a society. Now that does not mean that everybody has got to be married. Jesus was not, Paul was not; many have not. But woe betide a man who thinks he does not need women, or a woman who thinks she does not need men. We need each other, not just in marriage but in society. There are complementary natures that need each other and if you are to understand God fully you need to look at men and women together. If you want to see his image, you need to look at both. In animals, male and female is simply a reproductive thing. It is not an image of God. But in Genesis 1 the male and female distinction in the human race is Godlike rather than animal-like. Again, I shall leave you to work out the implications.

Number 8. What God says to man he does not say to any other creature. Now he did say to the fish and fowls to increase, multiply, fill, and he said the same to man. But then he went on to say to man, "And I put you in charge of all the other creatures." He never said that to any animal. But to man he says, "You are to subdue. You're in charge; you're in control." That sets man apart from the animals.

Number 9. Man's food is to be different from animals' food. Man is to eat the fruit of the tree; the leaves are for the animals – or literally, the *grass* is for the animals. I will tell you two stories to underline this. King Nebuchadnezzar, that great ruler of Babylon who got so big-headed that one night as he walked through the gardens – the hanging gardens which were one of the seven wonders of the world on top of his palace – he said, is not this great Babylon my kingdom which I have built by my power and for my glory. He had his own version of the Lord's Prayer which was mine is the kingdom, the power and the glory. And God put his hand on that man and a few days later he was stark, staring mad. And it says, his nails grew long and his hair grew long just like Howard Hughes in his last days. And it says,

CREATION

he was eating grass like the cattle, as much as to say, that is what he sank to.

A friend of mine is a missionary in India and he said that one of the most awful things that happened to him was when he was sitting down for his meal one day with his wife and he looked out of the door and there was a poor Indian man dressed in rags with a few children hanging on to his hand coming up the path to the bungalow door. And this Indian knocked at his door and said to my friend, "Please could my children graze your lawn?" And this Indian was so desperate to get food for his children that he wanted them to come and get down and eat the grass. And my friend said, something went right through him; they were so hungry they were ready to do it. And when he saw children getting down and grazing, he just could not face it.

You see, there is some profound distinction here. Can you feel it? Now giving somebody fruit from your fruit tree – you wouldn't think twice about children doing that. But seeing them graze your lawn, how would you feel? God made a distinction between animals and men, even in the food line. We do not graze like animals.

And the tenth distinction was that God gave man a week to be his cycle of activity. Now, that is not a natural division. No animal or bird observes the week. Nature observes lunar months – by the moon; and solar years – by the sun. It never observes weeks. I wished they had when I used to get up at four in the morning and milk 90 cows every morning before breakfast. They didn't observe Sunday at all. And I can remember falling asleep in the pew of the church again and again because I had been up doing all that work and I wished the cows would take a day off but they never observed a week. Animals have no concept of the week or the weekend. It is purely a spiritual thing for man. "The Sabbath was made for man," and it links him with God not the animal world. And the whole concept of the week, mark my words, vanishes if God vanishes from society. And you will

Chapter 3: The origin of man

lose your Sunday fairly quickly as Britain becomes more pagan. It is one of the things that marks us out from the animals. The animals don't have a week but we do because on the seventh day God rested and said, now if you're going to be human, you will need one day in seven to rise above what animals do – make a living. You 'll need to rise above just eating, drinking and marrying and getting your food. And you'll need to be human and remember who you are one day a week. But the week is built into us. We take a week normally, don't we? We just assume it is normal, but no animal ever did. So, in these 10 ways, add all those 10 things up and you get an equation which says that man is not an animal. And that is just in a handful of verses in the Bible. And we have found at least 10 differences.

We now turn to Genesis 2. And the first thing we have got to say is that many people say Genesis 2 is a second, alternative account of creation and that it has come from a different source, and that you can take your pick but it is written so differently that they are almost contradictory. Have you heard this? Well now, I want to show you that that is not so. They are very different in style, in order, in range, in viewpoint. But they are complementary; they are not alternatives, they are supplements. They are looking at the same story from two angles. Now this is often God's way in the Bible. In fact, to portray Jesus he had to give us four angles on Jesus – Matthew, Mark, Luke and John. God does not mind repeating himself, but usually, through the Bible, he tells you a thing twice. Right through the Old Testament he often gives us two accounts of the same thing from different angles so we get the picture.

Now, I hope you never have a mug shot in the police station, but if they ever get you, they will take two shots. And in one you will have one ear and in the other you will have two ears. And somebody could say, "Well, I think he only has one ear," and some could say, "Well, I think he has two." But in fact, you need the two shots to get a full picture of the man, so if you get

CREATION

your mug shot, that is what you will get.

And Genesis 1 and Genesis 2 are two snapshots, two "movie films" of creation. And I just want to show you the contrast of viewpoint between these two. They have a different view of God and they a different view of man. And funnily enough, on both they are the opposite way around. In chapter 1, God is like man because man is like God, but in chapter 2 God is very different from man. In chapter 1, man is like God but in chapter 2 man is very unlike God. And in fact, both are true and if you want a full picture of God and man, it is not enough to say God is like man without saying God is also unlike man. And it is not enough to say man is like God because it is also true that he is unlike God. And it is as if God has given us two different viewpoints to give us the whole truth, and balance it out.

Do you ever shut your eyes after you have read a portion of the Bible and ask, where are you standing? I don't think many do. For example, you know when you read that parable of the Pharisee up at the front of the temple saying, "I thank thee that I am not as other men are"; and the man at the very back of the temple beating his breasts and saying, "God be merciful to me a sinner," do you know that story? When you read that story where do you stand? Where do you look to see the man at the back and where do you look to see the man at the front? If you are like me, you say, "Well, I'm neither," so I put myself halfway down, and mentally I find myself looking at the man up front and looking back at the man at the back. Do you see what I mean? You place yourself.

Now, as I read Genesis 1, I feel that I am just below the clouds; I am up in the air and watching it happen. Do you see what I mean? When I read Genesis 1, I find myself looking down at the dry land appearing and looking at the clouds, and I find myself hovering above the surface of the earth. If you think a bit, I think you will find that is where you find yourself looking. But you have probably never thought about it so you never realised it.

Chapter 3: The origin of man

But you are hovering above the thing. But you are not up where God is and you are not down on the surface of the earth; you are watching it from just a bit out, right? Do you realise that is where the Holy Spirit was while it was all happening. He was hovering above the waters. And it was the Holy Spirit who conveyed Genesis 1 to man and so you find yourself exactly where he was. Does that make sense to you?

Well, in Genesis 2, where do you find yourself? Hiding behind a tree, right? Your feet are on the ground in Genesis 2, right? You read it through and you will find yourself in the garden and your feet are on the ground; you are not hovering up, looking down at it. The viewpoint is of someone in the garden, which is precisely where Adam was, and since we get this from Adam now – he was not around in Genesis 1 so he could not tell us but he was round in Genesis 2 and has clearly passed on – we have his viewpoint; we have switched from the divine to the human viewpoint. We have switched from where the Spirit was hovering to where Adam was walking and in fact we are just round the back of a tree listening in on the conversation. That is where you are, and that is the viewpoint. Now from those two viewpoints you will get the whole truth – from the divine and the human. You will see the real truth and from the divine viewpoint, man is like God, not the animals. But from the human point of view, down here on earth, we are much more like the animals than God. Do you follow? That is what we feel because we are down here and we are in the same environment.

Now that difference of perspective is very important because with Genesis 2 we begin history and geography. We begin the actual events of the story of our human race and the places are now actual, literal places with names. And one of the biggest differences of all between Genesis 1 and Genesis 2 is that both God and man now have names. As long as it was just God and his world, there was no intimacy, no relationship that needed names because the world did not talk to God and God did not talk to

CREATION

the world directly. He spoke to his Spirit. But now in Genesis 2 there are relationships. And now names are needed and one of the first things you must have noticed is that whereas in Genesis 1 it is God said, God saw, in Genesis 2 it is LORD God did and LORD God saw. And that word LORD in capital letters is a bit of a mistranslation. They have just put it there wherever there is a strange list of four letters in the Hebrew – JHVH. And since most English people don't know how to pronounce Hebrew, they usually say Jehovah. So, when an Englishman says Jehovah, the Hebrew does not know what he means and when the Hebrew says Yahweh, the Englishman does not.

It is interesting that the Jerusalem Bible, the Roman Catholic, does put Yahweh in there, and that is God's name. "God" is not a name, it is a title; it is a description. But Yahweh is a name. It is as if you say, "Oh look at baby George." Now "baby" is not a name. That tells you *what* he is, but George tells you *who* he is. Do you understand? Or if you say, "Our shop steward, Joe." Now, shop steward tells you what he is but Joe tells you who he is, right? And "God" does not tell you who God is, it tells you what he is. But LORD tells you who he is. And it is a strange name. It comes from the verb to be, and we are not quite sure whether it is a participle or the root of the verb or what but it just means "being", "is", "am". I do not know quite how to translate it. I just translated it "the God Who Is". It is almost as if God says, my name is "is", but since that sort of sounds a little silly to us, let us just go a little further and use the translation maybe that is used in many English versions – "I Am". That is why they tried to stone Jesus when he called himself that. It means, I've always been here; I always will be here; whatever else exists, I will always exist. The world wasn't always here, you weren't always here, but I was. I Am. I am the God who *is*. So, when you want to refer to me, you refer to me as "Is", the God who is – I Am!

A tremendous name, and it means that now I can have a

Chapter 3: The origin of man

personal relationship with him, but notice that it is not an equal relationship. In an equal relationship, you give each other names, but in this relationship, God gives himself his name and he gives us our name. It is a bit one-sided in a sense. It is the relationship of a superior to an inferior, and we need to remember that all the time. We should not get pally with the Deity. We should remember always that, though we are his sons, and he has told us to call him Dad, he never says that we are equals and we never will be so we really must watch this.

So, he gives himself his name, I Am, the God Who Is, and he gives us our name. He says, "Hello Dusty." That is what Adam means. It is a nickname and nicknames always describe the person, have you noticed? "Ah, fatty"? You know? It describes him, doesn't it? Oh, here comes old Miserable. Nicknames describe, and Adam simply means Dust Or else, you could call him Clay. Hello Clay, I'm just going to call you Dusty. Later, Adam called his wife Lively so they were quite a pair – Dusty and Lively.

But I want to convey to you the real meaning of the names. We tend, you know, to put a halo round biblical names and put them in a stained-glass window, saying *Adam*, you know? Dusty? It is a constant reminder to him of his place. I am the God who is. Hello Dusty. I got you from the dust and that's where you're going back. "From dust we come and to dust we shall return."

Well, that is chapter 2 on God. Now look at chapter 2 on man. And if chapter 1 emphasises man's difference from the animals, chapter 2 emphasises his similarity. In fact, everything it says about the creation of man in chapter 2 is identical with what is said about the animals, but I am afraid that is often misinterpreted, especially by that dreadful word *soul*, as if somehow God put something very special called a soul into man. In fact, the Hebrew – you must take my word for it – it says exactly the same about man as it says about all the animals. And it only says two things in Genesis 2 about man.

CREATION

The first thing is that has made out of the ground, meaning that every particle in his body came from the soil. There is not a single thing in my body that you cannot find in the ground somewhere. And it says twice that out of the ground he made the animals, so I have exactly the same origin as the animals in that they and I came out of the soil; and that is where we came from. So, God took of the dust of the earth; that is what he did with the animals too. He is saying, you're not so different. You're the same as the animals; I'm treating you the same way.

And the second thing that is said here is that God breathed into Adam – quite literally gave him the kiss of life, and from his mouth to Adam's nostrils he just filled his lungs with air and Adam became a living creature, which is the identical Hebrew that is applied in Genesis 1 to all the animals – living beings. So that in fact Genesis 2 says exactly the same about man's creation as about the animals'. So, whereas chapter 1 says man and the animals are quite different, chapter 2 says man and the animals are exactly the same. And you will not understand man until you put those two things together because that is where we are, that is where we came from. We came from the same place as the animals but we are quite different and that explains the contradiction, the inconsistencies, the tensions we feel.

We know basically that we are the same as animals. We breathe the same air. We have the same kind of blood circulation as every other mammal. We bring our young to birth the same way as every other mammal. We know that, and yet I know deep down that I am not an animal. I am not; I am different. So, it is a contradiction and a tension and we have to live with it.

Notice that at first there was only one man and a male one, and if you have problems about God producing life from the dust then I am sorry but you might just miss it happening to you one day because resurrection is nothing more than that. And whenever I stand at a graveside when I am conducting a funeral and say, "dust to dust, ashes to ashes, dust to dust; in sure and certain hope

Chapter 3: The origin of man

of the Resurrection to eternal life", I feel like saying to myself, if I can't believe that God made Adam out of dust, then how can I believe that this body will ever be resurrected from the dead?

So you see the whole creation/resurrection thing is all tied up. If you have problems with one you are going to have problems with the other. And if you cannot believe that God did it for Adam then I question whether you really believe in your own resurrection coming down the line. Because God will really have a bigger problem then than he had with Adam, to get your dust together and to get it breathing again, but that is what we say at the funeral service. Let me just outline for you now what we are going to cover in the rest of this chapter more briefly. Because man is this funny mixture and has this dual origin, being a hybrid, a creature of heaven and earth, a creature both divine and human, both like the animals and unlike them, like God and unlike him, it means that he has certain very tricky relationships to get into. And we are just going to look at four relationships that he has to have because he is this dual creature. We are going to look at his relationship with the plant life, with vegetation. Then we will look at his relationship to God, going to the other extreme. Then we will come back and look at his relationship to the animal world and then finally, we will look at his relationship to other human beings. At each of these four levels man will have a unique relationship because he is what he is. And getting those relationships right is the secret of feeling at home in God's world.

Now, the first relationship is vegetation. Genesis 2 suddenly goes back to day 3 and says that the earth was not originally a very hospitable environment. There were no plants – wild plants – and no cultivated herbs and the reason was there was no rain to irrigate and there was no man to cultivate so you got neither wild plants nor cultivated. That was what it looked like, pretty barren. And you know, when the astronauts came back from the moon and got nearer to the earth, they said that the most exciting

CREATION

colour that they saw was the colour green because they had not seen anything green out in space. And the vegetation of earth – this is a green planet and we ought to be jolly thankful it is. But there was a time when it was not; there was not a blade of grass, there was not a single herb anywhere. And then God set about putting that right. The first thing was to get some water in there, and the second one was to get the man in there to cultivate it. And so he began to do it.

From now on, attention focuses on only part of the earth. There is a sense I get that God let the plants spread naturally, spontaneously, randomly over most of the earth, but in one part he placed them. That is the sense we get. That therefore you would expect if you had been around then, that most of the earth would be as randomly vegetated as it is now so that seeds just would fly around in the wind, settle and grow and the dandelion grows here and the sycamore there. But in one place God decided to prepare a park. I much prefer that word to garden. The word garden conveys to me flower beds and things and that is not what is meant, but the word *park* conveys exactly what is meant – a very carefully planted place that would have two qualities, not only to contain trees that were useful but an arrangement of them that was beautiful. Which tells you this, that man needs an aesthetic as well as a utilitarian environment. Do you understand what I am saying? It is not just enough to have a useful place to live in; man needs an attractive place to live in. I wish all architects could hear that. But I saw an allotment where, among the potatoes the man had planted pansies and I thought, good for you, you've made a human place. The old cottage gardens in the Middle Ages had the vegetables among the flowers so that you had a useful *and* an attractive place. And there are some gardens that are jolly attractive but no earthly use. There are some gardens that are very useful, all nice straight rows of peas, but they are not attractive. And God made a park that was both for man.

Chapter 3: The origin of man

For the animals, it was random planting. It did not need to have beauty. For man, it needed to. Now that says something to me about the environments we create for each other. Our architecture, the town planning. I would like to get hold of the town planners who planned Basingstoke, or certainly parts of it, and say, "Did you realise that man needs an attractive as well as a utilitarian place to live?" When I see people pushed into these high-rise flats in rabbit hutches, my soul protests. That may be utilitarian but it is not aesthetic. And so God said for the animals, nature can look after itself because an animal does not stop and say, "'Hey, what a sunset." But man does. And so God made a parkland and it was called "Delight" or in Hebrew "Eden". The park of delight, what a beautiful ring that has. I prefer that to The Garden of Eden. The Delightful Park, that was where man was brought after he was made. And man was brought to it to do two things to it. He was told, develop it and protect it, and therein lies the whole seed of ecology.

I love the word *husbandry*. My first degree was in agriculture and it was called husbandry, Animal Husbandry, Land Husbandry. It is a beautiful word, isn't it? In other words, man is to be a husband to nature, he is to develop it, yes; put his own mark on it, yes; but it must always be to protect it. The trouble is we have often put our mark on nature and destroyed it. Like the dust bowls of Central America. Man is to develop and protect it and I would love to stay with that and just preach about ecology because all the modern cry for ecology is rooted and grounded in Genesis chapter 2. That is to be his relationship. He is free to change the shape of nature, he is free to put his own pattern on it, he is free to make farms and fields. He is free to do that, but woe betide him if he does not protect it at the same time, if he takes out more than he puts in – that is bad husbandry.

By the way, that Park of Delight was a particular geographical location on a map. It is not a myth. It was a real place. It was somewhere in the mountains of Armenia north of Mesopotamia

CREATION

because at least two of the rivers are still there. The other two probably went north to the Caspian and the Black Sea. But the two that are still there, the Tigris and Euphrates, their headwaters are right up in those Armenian hills, that is where the park was, so let us get rid of this myth idea. Why would God tell us where it was if it is a myth? Why would he give us names that we still have if it is all a myth? And there are even hints about the land around it. There was gold here and onyx there and those have been found. Havilah is to the east of Armenia; Cush was to the north between the Caspian and the Black Sea. So we are into real geography, real history, real events.

Now, the second relationship that I want to touch on is the relationship between man and God. So, I now come to the relationship with God and those two unusual trees. Because that is when people think you are back into myth again. Right in the middle of the park were two fruit trees and one had the capacity to lengthen your life – indefinitely – and the other had the capacity to shorten it very quickly. That is significant. God put man in a place where eternal life could be his and where he could die like the animals.

Now let us look at those two trees together first. Were they magical trees? There is certainly no tree around now with fruit like that. No, they were not magical trees. They were ordinary fruit trees but they were *sacramental trees*. Now I wonder if you know what I mean by that. Let me tell you. In the sacrament of the Lord's Supper, it is ordinary bread and ordinary wine yet you could be very ill and even die as the result of taking it. There is nothing magical about the bread and the wine. There is nothing poisonous in them but Paul said that if you eat that bread and drink that wine without discerning the Body, then you can eat and drink damnation and judgment to yourself. And he said that is why some of you are sick and some have even died, and we should remember that when we take bread and wine. It is a serious thing.

Chapter 3: The origin of man

Now, there is nothing magical about the bread and the wine but God has appointed the eating of that bread as a sacramental act which carries certain spiritual effects and which even carries physical effects. Do you see what I mean by sacramental as distinct from magical? The trees are not magical. They are sacramental. They are not weird and wonderful trees, it is just that God says that eating that tree will bring you life, physical life, as eating the bread and drinking the wine wrongly at Communion can bring you death – sacramental. There is nothing more to these trees than that they are sacramentally appointed. The water in baptism is simply H2O, and yet what can't it wash away? And we know what it can wash away because it is *sacramental*. It is not magic in the water, but God has appointed that act of being immersed as a means of grace. Now are you following me? So, the two trees were not magical or mythical. They were two trees that God *appointed* for certain purposes and said that in the act of eating this is what I've tied to that act. So, they are sacraments, one of life, one of death.

Now let us look a little more closely. The tree of life simply means this, that man by himself would not live forever but that the possibility of him doing so was before him. And God was saying that sacramentally that's what I'm offering you; that if you are without that, then you will die like the animals but you are capable of receiving a life that will go on and on. And still it is true that I am capable of receiving everlasting life from God. I do not have it in me. I am not immortal but "this mortal can put on immortality". I am capable of living forever. But it is not inherent in me. I have to eat. I have to take something from God to make that possible. Do you follow me? Now that is what the trees stood for. And there are other exciting things that I could go on to say but there was just one thought I wanted to get hold of there. You know, there is no reason why my body should die. It is an incredible machine that is capable of replacing any cells in it that wear out. In fact, every seven years I change every

CREATION

cell. And the question arises, why can't that just go on? Do you know, there is no scientist who has yet been able to discover why the clock begins to wind down. Theoretically this is a self-perpetuating machine and yet it is not. Why can the body not just go on, replacing itself when hair falls out, growing new hair, when skin falls off growing new skin? Because I do that regularly. And when I am in my prime, I am pretty good at it but I am afraid I am already into the losing end of the battle. Every time I go to the dentist or the barber, I realise I am on the losing end of the battle now. Now why should my body begin to wear out?

There is no scientific reason why your body should die, none at all. It is not really a natural event, and you know, that is why the human being says, "I'm not made to die; I hate death." If there is one phobia that people have, it is about death. If there is one unmentionable five-letter word, it is d-e-a-t-h. And we kick against it, we rebel against it, we dress it up like a harvest festival, we refer to people *passing away* or *passing on*, and I have noticed that when I say to people, so-and-so has died, they almost jump. If I had said, passed away, that would have been fine, but they've died? No. And we hate it, we kick against it because, as one text in the Bible says that God has set eternity in our hearts. And that is why the Russians are looking for the elixir of life. They know we are made for a longer life than we get. Every one of us feels that life is too short for all the things we have hoped for and dreamed about and want to do. And God says, that he has put that in your heart and put a tree of life within your reach. And you can have everlasting life, but you don't have it – you must appropriate it. Which means that I am capable of receiving it.

So, what could prevent me from receiving it? Well, eating from the other tree. And what is eating from the other tree? What does it mean, this tree of knowledge of good and evil? Well, the word "knowledge" in Scripture does not mean head knowledge, it means experience knowledge. It means having

Chapter 3: The origin of man

a personal involvement with something. "So Adam *knew* his wife Eve and she conceived and bore a son." Now that is not knowing about someone. That is intimately relating. And the tree of knowledge is simply this. It stands for wanting to experience evil as well as good, and even more deeply, God is saying is this: the condition of your living forever is that you keep your innocence and you only keep your innocence through obedience. Or in other words, you cannot keep your innocence by trying things out for yourself but by trusting someone else to tell you what is good and what is evil.

I am trying to spell this out very simply. Let me do it this way. A girl can keep her virginity only by refusing to experience sex before marriage and therefore by trusting someone to tell her it is wrong to do so. But if she says, "I'm going to try it and see if it really is as bad as people tell me," she will lose her innocence and she can never regain it. Therefore, she cannot ever choose to be innocent again, do you follow me? I was glad to see that the present Miss World and the previous one have both chosen to be virgins at the time of their marriage and neither are married yet. It is quite a new thing for Miss Worlds to be saying this. They have chosen that on the authority of someone else. In both cases, they were brought up in Godly homes and they were told it is wrong. They have accepted the judgement of someone else and they are keeping their innocence and they will be able to present it at their marriage, which is the best wedding present a bride can give her husband. Now, if they once say, "No, I'm going to try both ways; I'm going to try chastity and unchastity and *I* will decide what's right and wrong for me," then I am afraid they cannot decide. They will inevitably lose their innocence through disobedience. Now, have I explained it fully?

And God says, you are free to eat any of the trees. I give you great liberty but I give you one restraint – that you leave me to decide what's right and wrong for you. And that you don't try to experience things to decide for yourself, then the whole garden is yours. There will be no loss of happiness through that one tree being restrained, none at all. But the one thing he says I warn you about is this – when you lose your innocence you cannot live forever because you will spoil my universe forever. Now does that all make sense? To me it is utter sense. Once a person is no longer innocent they inevitably spoil the rest of their life. They can never be back where they were again. Now that means God says that innocent people can live forever; they will be a sheer joy. They will enjoy everything; but if *you* start sampling things you shouldn't, and if you do it because you want to decide what's right and wrong because you want the personal knowledge of both and make your own decision, then I'm afraid I have to decide at that point that you die. Therefore, death to the human being is a judicial and not a natural event. Do you follow me in that?

It is not something that would have happened naturally to the human race. It is a *sentence* of death. That is why we loathe it; that is why we hate it because we know there is something moral in there. The sting of death is sin. That is what spoils it. There is something moral concerned with this. We know we were not made to die; we feel instinctively that God should be letting us live forever. And we are right in that; he wanted to but he had to put that restraint because he said, the people I want to live forever are innocent people who can really enjoy my world and will not spoil it. And anybody who spoils it must live temporarily and not permanently. Now that makes a whole lot of sense to me and we shall see when we study Chapter 3 just what went wrong. For this universe is out of order, that is for sure. But those were the conditions. They are not hard conditions. It does mean that the first commandment God gave to men that was a moral commandment did include the word *not* in it and God does say, "Thou shalt not" but he does it for our own good, for our enjoyment.

Now, every parent has the same dilemma. Your children grow up and you want to tell them, don't touch that; don't get into

Chapter 3: The origin of man

drugs; don't do this; don't do that. And your children feel that you want them to live a miserable, narrow, spoiled life. You are doing it because you want them to keep their innocence and enjoy the good things that God has made, right? That is why you are doing it. And every earthly father has that dilemma with his own children. If only they would decide to trust and obey and keep their innocence. But knowing your own heart you feel your own children will to a degree do what you did and say, "I'm going to try it for myself."

I can remember the first cigarette I had in the bushes. I was sick as a dog. I was eleven. And I could take you to the bushes now where I ploughed my way through that. Morbid when I think of it. Oh, lost weekend. I regretted it. Why was it in the bushes? Because I had been told not to, and I was going to try it. It had one blessed effect. I have never wanted to touch the things since. But I am sure that I lost my innocence and it spoiled something. And you can never wipe that out of your memory or your personality. You can never recover your innocence. I know what it is like to smoke. I cannot ever say I don't.

This was God, and he looked down at this beautiful park and the beautiful person he put in it and he said, I just want you to stay innocent in that park. That's why I put that tree there because I'm going to be the Lord. I'm going to be the boss. I will decide what's right and wrong. But it's for your enjoyment, it's for your good. Will you trust me? If you don't, then I have to warn you, I'm not going to let you spoil this park because innocent people don't spoil things; guilty people do.

Well now, that was his relationship to God and it is very clear. Only to man did God give such a choice. Only to man did God say, now you're responsible for your own life as well as the plants and the animals. And I think you do not treat a man as a human being if you do not treat him as a responsible being. I have sat in courts where people have pleaded that the man in the dock is a poor, innocent victim of his heredity and his environment and

CREATION

that he is sick and he needs a psychiatrist, he is not responsible for his actions. And I feel you are not treating that man as a man. You are treating him as a machine. And God says that you are a human being, you are responsible for your choices. You are responsible. And you treat a man as a man when you treat him as responsible.

Now, the third relationship is the relationship to the animals. The relationship to the plants was to develop them and protect them but not to have any more than that. And I was sad, on the TV, to see a man who had 8,000 cacti in his semi-detached house. And when he was asked why did he have so many – they crowded every inch of his little semi – and when the interviewer said, "Why do you have so many?" He said, "Well, it's something to talk to at night." And you know, I felt the hurt of God's heart in that. I felt God saying, I didn't make you to talk to A cactus. It's almost as sad when you find a dear old lady who has no relationships except with a cat or a budgie. That is against the will of God. And it is sad. It may not be their fault but it is not God's will. So, the plants, they are there to serve man, to provide food, but they are not to be in a relationship. And if they do get into that position, then there is a distortion of real life.

The second group are the animals. Now, there is to be a closer relationship between man and animals. He is to give them names and to give a name is to express power and authority over a person. That is why school children love to give their teachers names. It gives them a feeling of some power. You know? Some getting back at them. But you see, giving a name means that you have authority over it. And so, God said to man, since you're in charge of the animals, I'm not going to name the animals. I named you Adam, but you're to name the animals.

I am sure you have heard that lovely story of Adam calling an animal a rhinoceros and Eve asking him, "Now why did you call that a rhinoceros?" "Well," he said, "have you ever seen anything that looked more like a rhinoceros than that?" Well, whatever

Chapter 3: The origin of man

his thinking behind the naming, in fact most of the names were descriptions and God said, now Adam, what do you say about this one? And what he said became its name and all the early names for animals are actually a description of what they look like or what they sound like. I give you some examples – cuckoo; and what you call a cuckoo is a description of its call so you just call it the cuckoo. And man gave all the names – hippopotamus, *hippos* is Greek for horse and *potamos* is Greek for river. And if ever you have seen a hippopotamus with its head just above water, you see a horse's head; and so it is called the horse of the river. And all the animals' names you can trace back to this. And man was in charge of the animals so he gave them names. Man is able to analyse, to describe, to label, to categorise; that gives him authority over them. To give a name is to have authority. Nicknames are authority. I cannot bear men being called numbers but you know, a prisoner comes under the authority of the prison authorities and the prison authorities say you are number 4509. They label that man and it gives them power over that man. They refer to him like that.

In marriage, the wife changes her name, and that is very significant. She changes from one man's name to another man's name, from her father's name to her husband's name because now she is related to the leadership of another man. It Is interesting to see that that custom is being attacked now as we get further from God's pattern.

But with animals, however much man names an animal – and we have not got round to naming our ducks yet but we named our guinea pig and we named our dog – it must not and cannot be a full companionship. And where any man, where a husband is fonder of his greyhound than his children, there is something outside of God's will. Do you know, if God was fonder of his pets and his garden than of his children, we would be in a sad state, wouldn't we? Did you know that every time you worry about anything, every time *I* worry about anything, I am libelling

CREATION

God. I am saying he cares more for his garden and his pets than he does for his children. Jesus said, "Consider the lilies of the field, how they grow; they toil not, neither do they spin". He said, "even Solomon in all his glory was not arrayed like one of these." And consider the birds of the air, how they're fed. Why then are you worried about tomorrow, what to eat or what to put on – you're saying God cares more for his garden and his pets than for me when you worry – quite a thought.

So, the man noticed these animals and he looked at them. He said, "Well that's a cat, that's a dog, that's a horse." There was one word he never used when he named the animals. He did not call one of them *companion*. Among all the animals there was not found a companion for him. And that is why no human being can finally find a fulfilling relationship with an animal or a bird. And if you find yourself closer to an animal than human beings then you need to seek God again. Or if you know someone like that maybe you need to ask God if you should be relating to them and breaking their loneliness. There are all sorts of other things that I could say here. This is one of the reasons why buggery is such an abomination to God. It is a relationship that is not right in his sight.

I come finally therefore to the human relationships. How does man relate to vegetables? How does man relate to animals? How does man relate to God? All those relationships are what I call vertical relationships, either to things below you or someone above you. Relationship to plants and animals are down, relationship to God is up, but man cannot be fully human without a horizontal relationship. I have heard some Christians say, "Well, I have a beautiful relationship with the Lord, that's all I need." There is something terribly missing from that person's life. It is all vertical, there is no horizontal. And so Adam could not find a horizontal relationship any way, could not find it with the animals, could not find it with God. Each of those is vertical, an up and down relationship with a superior and an inferior. To the

Chapter 3: The origin of man

animals, he was superior, to God inferior, but not an equal. And poor old man, as he watched the animals come and named them, he noticed they always came and went in twos. They seemed to get on very well together and he felt very lonely. Why can't I have a mate like they all seem to? And God said that it is not good for a man to be alone.

Have you read *Robinson Crusoe*? He got life well organised on his desert island and he got really nicely settled in but he was a lonely man and one day he saw a human footprint on the beach as Man Friday and his loneliness was over. But that did not happen to the real Robinson Crusoe, who was a Baptist deacon from Largo in Scotland, Alexander Selkirk, and it was on his life that *Robinson Crusoe* was based. Daniel Defoe knew that Baptist deacon and that Baptist deacon was on a ship and he was cast off on a desert island for four years. He had his Bible with him and many of the things that you read in Robinson Crusoe happened to Alexander Selkirk. The one thing that did not happen was that there was no other human being and he was desperately lonely. If you go to Largo in Scotland you will see a statue outside the Baptist church up there. "It's not good for a man to be alone." And so God said, he's got vertical relationships with me, with the animals, but no horizontal ones.

And now comes the most tender and beautiful story. Man was never meant to be a soloist or a lone ranger. And here we have the first wedding and the first surgery under anaesthetic, a glorious story. We will finish the chapter with this. The origin of woman; she was a special creation, not from the dust like the man but from man. Now frankly that certainly won't fit in with evolution. She was made out of man but our modern scientific discoveries are showing how possible it is. In 1967, in Oxford, a scientist discovered that one cell taken from the body of a toad, not from its genital organs, but just from its skin or part of its gut, I think, one cell, he discovered actually had in it the tape, the genes for the whole body. It was a unique discovery because it means that every cell of my body could produce my whole body and if a cell just produces a kidney, it is because in the tape in that cell everything else but the kidney is switched off, and the kidney bit is allowed to operate. So that, from one cell, you can actually produce a whole body and from that cell in Oxford in 1967 that man produced an entire toad. It was a twin of the toad, or a *clone* as he called it, of the whole toad. Without any sexual relationship at all, that cell was made into a total toad. One cell! Every cell in my body contains the whole of my body on tape, that little DNA code contains the whole thing. What a discovery!

Now the word *rib* does not occur in the Hebrew. It just says part of the side of Adam, some tissue from his side, and God would simply clone Adam and do what they did in Oxford in 1967, take part of the tissue and produce a twin. The only bit of little genetic engineering he would need to do would be to change the Y chromosome into an X chromosome. That is the tiniest, tiniest little thing. It just needs a little extra arm on it and since each cell in my body is enough, not to produce a male body only, but a female as well, again certain things would be suppressed and certain things developed. All God would need to do would be to take a bit of tissue from Adam's side, change that one chromosome and Adam's had his operation under an anaesthetic. But boy, that must be a nice thing to come out of an operation to face, mustn't it? Now, why did God produce woman that way? Well, to say that man is incomplete now. He always will be incomplete as a lone ranger. He needs to be complemented with another life.

And in fact, when you married people make love, just remember, you are putting together again what God separated. That is what it is all about. That is why a man will find this the strongest relationship in his life, stronger even than his relationship with his parents, which is the strongest we have in the first 20 years of our life. But we are prepared to break that and to leave father and mother and cleave to someone we feel is completing us where they could not. And it all goes back to God cloning Adam and producing an identical twin who was female. And Adam, whether he had seen his own reflection in a pond or not, I don't know, but when he looked at Eve, he said, "This is it!" That is literally the translation. "This is it!" This is all there in the Hebrew; it is a lovely thing. And if you can imagine, since she was his twin, here were Adam and Eve looking at each other, same features, made for each other, made *from* each other. And knowing they just had to be one. It is an amazing thought.

And from that comes the whole of our thinking about marriage. Whenever Jesus got into arguments about divorce he would always come back to this part of the story and appeal to what happened from the beginning. Here is the basis. Every wedding you go to this is where it started. Here is a lovely comment by a saint called Matthew Henry. He said that when God made woman, he did not take her out of man's head to lord it over him, nor out of his feet to be trampled on by him, but out of his side to be equal with him, from under his arm to be protected by him and from near his heart to be loved by him. That is quite a sermon, isn't it? A beautiful comment.

Let me just tell you 12 things about marriage that are all here, and I just give them to you in sentences.

1. Sex is good, it is beautiful. God made it and he said that it is very good. Don't you ever libel God in that.

2. It is for partnership before it is for parenthood. That has a whole implication for contraception, but when God made sex he did not make it in man primarily to have children, but for man to have companionship. Therefore, making love is not primarily to have children. That is a profound thing to say. It is primarily as a sacrament of love. It is an expression of we belong to each other.

3. Man is incomplete by himself and needs a complementary partner. That is why the language like "my better half", "my other half", and "my alter ego" all make sense.

4. Man was prior to the woman but is not superior. In Genesis

1, man and woman both are in the image of God. Spiritually they are equal; functionally they are not, but spiritually they are. In value, status, everything, both are in the image.

5. God's pattern for marriage is monogamy: one man marries one woman. Therefore, polygamy – many wives – or polyandry – many husbands – are not God's will. I love the schoolboy who said, "To be married to one person for life is monotony." He nearly got it right. It is monogamy, alright?

6. Marriage has a legal and social side as well as a physical. There is an official leaving one home and cleaving to start another. Therefore, it is not just enough to say, "We're going to live together; what's marriage, it's just a bit of paper; it's just a legal fiction." It is very important that marriage is to be seen as a social as well as a physical thing. You are actually breaking certain relationships and entering into others and therefore a wedding is proper. It is right that it should be recognised by society, that this woman is not under the authority of her father now but under her husband. There is a leaving and a cleaving. And the father of the bride saying, "I give this woman to this man" is as important as the physical consummation. Therefore, all this talk about, you know, it's only a bit of paper, that is ridiculous in God's sight. It is a social as well as a personal and physical thing.

7. Cleaving is the physical consummation, two bodies becoming one again is the actual seal of the marriage. And that is why most laws recognise a nullity of a marriage that has not been consummated. So does the Bible.

8. Marriage takes precedence over all other relationships. A person's first duty is to their marriage partner and all the jokes about in-laws have some truth in there. Where the mother or father of either partner is having more influence on that partner than the other partner, there is something seriously wrong. And if a couple are finding themselves in that because the mother-in-law or father-in-law lives nearby, I would advise that couple to move house and to get away because the marriage relationship

Chapter 3: The origin of man

must take precedence over all others. "A man shall leave his father and mother."

9. Marriage is permanent. There is no divorce. When Jesus was asked about divorce, he referred people right back to the beginning and cleaving together, which means *holding on*. From the very first word of the Bible, loyalty is a vital ingredient of love and all thinking about separation must start with Genesis 2.

10. The husband is the leader of the marriage – not the dictator but the leader. He has that responsibility and it is expressed in the fact that he gives the name to his wife. Right from Genesis 2, Adam named her. And when we married my wife took my name. I gave my name to her, so it is not a democracy of two, neither is it a dictatorship of one. It is a leadership of three in which the husband is the head of the wife and Christ is the head of the husband. And I think a wife who has a husband whose head is Christ will be willing to accept him as her head. It is only when he is not under Christ that he will become a dictator.

11. The primary function of a wife is to help her husband. She is to be a helper. It is not two people with totally independent careers and ambitions sharing one house because it is cheaper and one bed because it is nice. Primarily – primarily – the wife is to be the helper of her husband and if she is God will enable her to find her fullest fulfilment in that very high calling.

12. The ideal in marriage is such complete freedom and ease with each other that you have nothing to hide. That last sentence is beautiful. They walked around with no clothes at all without the slightest embarrassment. In other words, neither of them distrusted the other; neither of them feared that anything they showed to each other would be abused or ridiculed. They were totally trusting. That of course has never been the same since and nudism cannot now be natural, nor ever will be again. In heaven we shall need clothes as we shall see next time.

Let me finish. We have seen an almost idyllic scene in Genesis 1 and 2 of man in a park of delight, of everybody in beautiful

CREATION

surroundings, of a marriage that is perfect. The whole thing. It is interesting that the Greek word for *park* is *paradisos*, from which we get Paradise, and when you read Genesis 2 you think, "Oh that must have been beautiful. It's a romantic dream. What went wrong?" Of the three major relationships, man's relationship below him to the creatures, alongside him to his companion and up to his Creator, those three relationships in which he would submit himself to the one above, submerge himself in the one alongside, and subdue those that were beneath, what went wrong?

One of those three went terribly wrong. Now, it is interesting that there is a whole new movement of people today who say the real thing that is wrong is our relationship to our environment and these people are devoting themselves to saving the whale and saving trees and you know the conservationist thrust there is. Some people are devoting their whole lives to trying to put man's relationship with nature right again. And then there are others who say, "No, that's not the key one; the key one is reconciliation with our fellow men, to stop destroying each other." The women at Greenham Common protesting, they are part of this, that the real thing that has gone wrong is the horizontal one, our attitudes to each other, the whole destructive alienation from each other.

The Bible's answer is that it was the one that went up that went wrong and that conservation is not the answer and reconciliation is not the answer at the human level. Salvation is the answer and that once that one goes wrong, the other two also go wrong. That if you are not rightly submitting to the Lord and letting him choose right and wrong and keep your innocence, then you cannot have a marriage in which you are unashamed in each other's presence. Nor can you have a relationship with God's creatures that will not get out of balance and will not be exploited, so that that is really preparing us for the very next stage in the story, the true story of the history of our race. Why are we living in a world out of order? Which relationship went wrong? And we will pick up the story in the next chapter.

CHAPTER 4:

SATAN EXPOSED

In this chapter we are going into Genesis chapter 3 And you will always hear it read at festivals of carols and readings and there is a reason for that and I hope you will see the connection between Genesis 3 and Christmas as I read a paraphrase to you. Now you know it so well in other versions so this may again just bring it home freshly to you.

"Now there was a deadly reptile around more cunning than any of the wild beasts that the God Who Really Is had made and he chatted up the woman. 'You don't mean to tell me that God has actually forbidden you to eat fruit from any of these trees?' She replied, 'No, that's not quite the situation; we can eat the fruit on the trees but God did tell us not to eat fruit from that one in the middle. In fact, he warned us that if we even touched it we'd have to die.' 'Surely he wouldn't do that to you,' said the reptile to the woman. He's just trying to frighten you off because he knows perfectly well that when you eat that fruit you would see things quite differently. In fact, you'd be in a position to rival him, able to decide for yourself what is good or bad for you.' So she took a good look at the tree and realised how nourishing and attractive the fruit appeared to be. Besides, it would obviously be an advantage to make one's own judgments so she picked it up, ate part and gave the rest to her husband to eat, which he promptly did. Sure enough, they did see things very differently. For the first time they felt self-conscious about their nudity so they tried to cover up by making crude clothes out of fig leaves.

"That evening they heard the approaching sounds of the God

CREATION

Who Really Is and ran to hide in the undergrowth. But the God Who Really Is called out to the man, 'What have you got yourself into?' And he replied, 'I heard you coming and I was frightened because I hadn't got any decent clothes so I'm hiding over here.' And he said, 'How did you find out that you were naked? Have you been eating the fruit I ordered you to leave alone?' The man said, 'It's all the fault of that woman you sent along. She brought this fruit to me so naturally I just ate it.' Then the God Who Really Is challenged the woman: 'What have you been up to?' The woman said, 'It's that awful reptile's fault. He deliberately fooled me and I fell for it.' So, the God Who Really Is said to the reptile, 'As a punishment for your part in this, above all the beasts I will curse your ways with a fate that is worse; on your belly you'll slither and thrust with your mouth hanging down in the dust. For the rest of the days of your life there'll be terror, hostility, strife between woman and you for this deed and you'll both pass it on to your seed but his foot on your skull you will feel as you strike out in fear at his heel.'

"Then to the woman he said, 'Let the pain of childbearing increase, the agony, labour and stress. Your desire for man never cool though the price will be that of his rule.' But to Adam he said, 'Because you paid attention to your wife rather than to me and disobeyed my order prohibiting that tree there's a curse on the soil. All the days you will toil. Thorns and thistles will grow among all that you sow. With a brow running sweat you will labour to eat then return to the ground in the state you were found as you came from the clay, you'll go back the same way.'

"Adam gave his wife a name, Eve. It means lifegiving because he realised that she would be the mother of all human beings who would ever live. Then the God Who Really Is made some new clothes from animal skins for Adam and his wife and got them properly dressed. And the God Who Really Is said to himself, 'Now that this man has become as conscious of good and evil things as we have been, how could we limit the damage if he

Chapter 4: Satan exposed

is still able to eat the fruit of the other tree and live as long as us?' To prevent this, the God Who Really Is banished him from the Park of Delight and sent him back to cultivate the very same plot of earth from which he had been moulded. After he had been expelled special angels were stationed on the Eastern border of the Park of Delight guarding access to that tree of continuous life with sharp and scorching weapons."

The world *is* out of order. There is something terribly, terribly wrong with it. In Genesis 2 you have got a picture of an idyllic place where anybody could be happy. There is a sense of joy, of peace. When you read Genesis 2 you just feel good and you understand why God looked at all that he had made and said, "That's very good." But I don't meet many people today who say the world is very good, do you? To quote one person – one man said to me, "The world's in a hell of a mess." And I said, "If you're using that word with the same meaning as I would use it, then you're absolutely right. Because hell is to be without God." And when you look at the present state of the world you say, that is surely not as it left God's hand; there's something terribly wrong about it. It is out of order.

Take just three very painful facts of our existence, three universal facts of human experience. Number one, our birth into this world is a painful process. It seems as if it is a struggle even to get in here. Did God plan birth to be like that originally? It is a strange bit of planning when you consider that the moment that starts that process is a moment of one of the most exquisite physical pleasures that we can know. And yet it leads to one of the greatest struggles a woman will ever know. And it is the woman who has the pain, not the man. And that seems a bit of bad planning; something is wrong in that. You would not have planned it that way, neither would I. Neither did God!

And that is just the beginning of this mortal existence, which is one big struggle for existence. Right through life it is a struggle to make ends meet. We are fairly well off in this country, we

CREATION

are fairly comfortable. And we don't realise that two-thirds of the babies born in the world today will not live to see maturity, never mind old age. And the whole human race is struggling to get enough food, struggling just to survive. And life is one big sweat. And we are in this strange tension that we want work and yet we don't; that we feel that if we are unemployed, we have lost our dignity, our identity, our self-respect; and yet if we get work, we find ourselves in such drudgery and struggle that sooner or later we get bored with it and we rebel against it; we want a change of job. And somehow, the work situation seems badly planned. But God did not plan it that way.

And when we get to the end of life, what a struggle it is to die for most people. It is a losing battle against the inevitable. And it is one of the most painful things. How each of us hopes that we will just be walking down the street and be gone. And a few people have that but the majority do not. And I think more people today fear dying than death. It is a struggle and if you have ever sat and watched it, it is a hard struggle to shake off this mortal clay for most people. Did God plan the world that way? No, he did not. It was not like that.

And I could just go on. But it is these things that make life one long painful struggle for the vast majority of people. Very few escape that struggle completely. That causes people to say, "This is not a good world. There's a lot of evil in it," and there is.

Now, it is fascinating to study pagan philosophies and myths at this point and find out how they explain what has gone wrong. Nearly every other religion and every other myth about the beginning of the world says that evil was always there. It was built in; it was part of our very existence. It always was, it always will be and you had better learn to live with it. That is the found in almost every other philosophy and religion in the world. It is fascinating to find out that the Bible utterly contradicts that and it says it was not always like this and it need not always be like this. Which, frankly, brings a ray of hope. It lifts your spirit to

Chapter 4: Satan exposed

know that once this world did not have a painful birth or a hard life or a struggle even to die, and that once none of those things applied, that God never intended a man to be an undertaker, that he never intended any plot of earth to be used for a cemetery. It was not in the plan and that is a revelation, and only God could have told us that because nobody else knew. But the implications of it are so far-reaching that it changes your whole outlook in life. Instead of becoming fatalistic you become full of faith.

Now, some believe that the world had built-in evil content from the beginning, and some religions say that is because there are two gods, one good and one bad and they were there from the beginning; or some even say there are 30,000,000 gods. The Hindu says that and some of them good and some of them bad, so that explains it all, doesn't it? And so you think, oh well that evil came from the bad one – a very simple explanation. But it is not true.

Then there are those who say, "Well, there's only one good god but he messed up the job of creating and somehow the material world has evil built into it and material matter is evil inherently. And it's because we live in a material world that there's evil in it." That again is absolute rubbish. When God made this material world it was good. The matter is good and physical life is good in God's sight, so we don't need to turn away from it as many religions do, and lie on a bed of nails. At the time of writing, there is even a Christian minister lying on a bed of nails as if he hadn't anything better to do than that. I hope he gets the point sooner or later.

Well, when I turn to the book of Genesis, I find it gives me certain clear insights into the problem of evil that we need to grasp, and here they are:

The first insight is that evil was not always in the world. Now, hold that firmly. When this world was originally made it was the best place you can imagine. It was heaven on earth; it was Paradise.

CREATION

The second thing is that evil did not *start* with man. Man was persuaded to get involved but evil did not start with the human being. Sin was not that original, so I am afraid we cannot even claim credit for that. We got persuaded to join in a conspiracy; that is the Bible insight as to how things went wrong. The evil came from outside us but it got inside us, that is the insight. We were originally good.

The third insight the Bible gives us I have already mentioned: evil is not something physical. It is not due to the fact that we live in a material world that it is evil. It is due to the fact that we live in a *moral* world that there is evil so we cannot blame our circumstances. We can only blame our *choices*. And that is a fundamental insight. And we will come back to it later because we live in a day when nobody wants to be responsible for themselves; when prisons are regarded as hospitals; when criminals are regarded as patients. And it is the mood of the day that we are *victims* of our circumstances. Well, you say that you were brought up like this. But too many people have risen above their circumstances and fallen below them to allow us to get away with that.

Evil is something that we choose; it is not forced on us by our circumstances. And Genesis 3 deals with this. Now just briefly Genesis 1 set the stage, Genesis 2 gave us the cast but with Genesis 3 the plot begins, and it is the first act in a drama that will last to the very last day of history. And it is the drama of how the world went wrong and how God is going to put it right. And that is the rest of the Bible in a nutshell. And so the plot begins with Genesis 3 and I mention again that it is real history and real geography. It is a place that you can put on a map and it was real people, Adam and Eve, and *you* were inside the body of those two people at the time.

I am amazed. Somebody has said that you could take the genes of all the existing human beings, the tiny genes that have controlled their body and you could get the world's genes into

Chapter 4: Satan exposed

a thimble. Now I cannot vouch for the truth of that but those tiny little genes that have made the shape of my nose and my height and the rest of it, you could put the whole world's genes into a thimble. But they were all in Adam's body once. And that is perhaps the most important thing that Genesis 3 will tell us because when you read Genesis 3, you suddenly feel that this is the story of my life. Have you ever felt that?

I remember a lad in the RAF came up to me once when I was a padre and he said, "I heard you speaking about Genesis 3." He said, "You don't believe that? Is that true?" I said, "Listen, if I put you in the library on camp here" – and there was a big library – "if I put you in that library and I told you, that there are books here on every subject you could be interested in and there are enough books for you to read for the next hundred years, but just watch out, there's one book on the top shelf that is not to be read by anyone under 25, but the rest – there are enough books on all the subjects you could possibly be interested in for you to read." I said, "What are you going to do if I leave you alone in that library?" And he said, "Okay Padre, I get the point." And off he went.

And when you read this chapter, you are reading yourself. You are looking into a mirror and in fact, the Bible itself says reading the Word of God is like looking into a mirror; don't forget what you see. Because that is utterly foolish to look in a mirror and then say, "I don't like the look of that," and forget. Because actually you will have to go on living with that look or other people will. So, you had better remember what you saw and put it right. I looked in the mirror and I suddenly thought yesterday morning, "I've forgotten my razor. I do shave a bit of my beard and I thought, I've forgotten my razor. I thought, how can I go to the meetings in Bristol looking like a tramp?" Now I could have said, "Oh I'm just going to forget what I saw," but it would not have dealt with it. Not at all. And when you read this chapter, it is like reading your own life story, with one exception. There

CREATION

is just one thing that is not true for us that was true for them.

But let us get into the story, and your first impression is that it is all a fairy story. Here is a serpent having a good old chat – and a pretty clever one too. It is not just the problem of a talking animal, it is the problem of a pretty intelligent, thinking animal. That is the biggest problem, not the talking but the brain behind it. I tell you, in less than 50 words he had tied up the human race in slavery. And a brain that can do that has really got some power. I certainly can't get through what I have got to say in 50 words, but Satan could. Now at first sight it seems like a just-so story of how the snake lost its legs, do you know what I mean? That is the kind of feel of it, and so people reading that just dismiss it as a fairy tale. But let us tackle that head-on. Let us deal with the first problem – how come a serpent is talking to a woman and so cleverly? Well, there are three possibilities and I just hand them to you and then I will tell you which one I believe.

The first possibility, and it is quite within the realm of God's capability, is that he actually created a highly intelligent animal who could think and talk. After all, he created you, so he could do it with an animal. But frankly I don't believe that is the explanation – he could have done that but I don't think that is the explanation.

At the opposite end is a second possibility, which ties in with the rest of the Bible. We have got the advantage of the rest of the Bible. Eve did not; she just saw an animal. But we read in the book of Revelation, "that old serpent the Devil called Satan". And so we have got the clue and we know it is something to do with Satan. So, could this be Satan in disguise? And Satan is clever enough to adopt any disguise he likes. He can come to you as an angel of light. In fact, if he did not disguise himself, you would probably have nothing to do with him. So, he is pretty clever; he always comes dressed up as someone or something else. And you will find that all the way through Scripture.

Have you seen the film *The Gospel According to St. Matthew*

Chapter 4: Satan exposed

directed by the Italian film director Pasolini? It is a brilliant film done by an atheist Communist; it is superb. But there is one moment that really shook me. Jesus was in the wilderness – a dreadful barren place – sitting there after six weeks looking gaunt, hungry, tired, all in. And the camera just pans round and there in the distance is a little cloud of dust getting nearer and nearer and you know it is the tempter coming. And he is kicking up the dust and you just see that cloud of dust coming and you think, what will he look like? How will he do it in the film? And then the dust only clears about 12 yards from the camera, and the shock. Do you know what that Communist made the Devil look like? He looked exactly like a broker in the stock exchange, very well dressed, nice suit, with a rolled umbrella, and suave, confident and looking down at this tired, hungry Christ with all the confidence. "My dear fellow, you look as if you could do with a good meal. Why don't you turn those stones..." It was so persuasive, so plausible, so real and you suddenly realised that you could meet a businessman in London and Satan could talk to you, you know? It was a marvellous piece of insight.

That is why Jesus even had to say to his closest friend, "Get behind me, Satan." He had to say it to Peter because Satan was getting at him through Peter and he can get at you through your wife, your husband, your children, through your nearest and dearest. He is not a fool to ring your front doorbell with a forked tail and horns. Neither do the angels come in white nighties with harps. If they did, how could you "entertain them unawares"? You need to realise that supernatural beings do not *appear* as that, and you could meet an angel this week. You could give a lift to them in your car – Christians do without realising. That is why you have got to be on your guard against the Devil. And this could be the Devil in disguise.

Another little point about getting in disguise. I was fascinated to read about a children's camp where they put on a Punch and Judy show and they decided to get a bit of Christian teaching

CREATION

across through the Punch and Judy show at the kids' camp. And so, they had a little figure, a red fiery Satan with a forked tail and you know Punch and Judy came and in came the Devil. And he told the children, "Put your tongue out at every adult you meet and don't wash your feet at night and leave banana skins for all the grown-ups to fall over." And do you know what happened? Those kids went out of their way to wash their feet, they picked up every bit of litter in the camp and the person who was doing this realised that because Satan was not in disguise, they just ran from him and subconsciously it had the very opposite effect on them. Isn't that interesting? Satan is no fool.

So, this could be Satan disguised as an animal, which would immediately take down any suspicion that Eve had because it was something within her existing experience, and that is how he usually comes. But I don't think that is the explanation. I give you a further one, which I believe is the true one, which is more difficult than those two, but I believe is probably the truth. And that is I want you to realise that animals can be possessed by both good and evil supernatural powers. I want you to realise that. Balaam's ass could speak because God's Spirit took hold of that ass.

When Jesus cast the demons out of the Gadarene demoniac, the swine rushed down the cliff into the sea and were drowned because the demons were in the swine. And I have had personal contact with a case in Switzerland where a possessed girl was dealt with and delivered and the sound out in the farm yard was terrible and they rushed out and found the pigs outside tearing each other to pieces because the minister delivering the person had said, "You demons go where the Lord Jesus sends you," and he sent them into the pigs again. And I think we need to realise that supernatural powers can take over any part of natural existence. And I believe that is what is happening here. I believe *both* Satan and an animal were involved and I will tell you why because something happened to the animals.

Chapter 4: Satan exposed

Did you know that every snake has legs – vestigial legs – which it cannot use. And the evolutionists of course have great fun with that. But you know, they are very near the truth. It did once have legs and they have shrivelled; they are no longer there. They are technically called vestigial organs or vestigial limbs. So that I believe the animal world was involved, but Satan is using an animal. Of course he would; you see that is within Eve's orbit. She knows trees, she knows animals, she knows birds. So, Satan said, now which part of creation shall I use to get through? And he chose a serpent.

Now, I saw a poster in Bristol of a pop group called Saints and Sinners. An advertisement for their latest album, and I forget the title now, but it is interesting, it was based on Genesis 3 and it is not a Christian group. And it showed a marble statue; you know, the statue of The Kiss with a man and a woman twined around each other in white marble. But something had been added on this album cover and it was a great big snake just approaching them. But you know that is wrong. It was not a snake that approached them. It *was* a reptile but with legs. Imagine something more like a lizard, I would think, a large lizard, a Nile Monitor – something like that, and you are nearer the mark. But almost every picture of Genesis 3 I have seen, I have seen a snake, have you? But coming to Adam and Eve it was not a snake. Something went wrong.

So, let us look at that. That means, by the way, that God did not create snakes originally, which I am thankful for. I feel that is right. I just cannot bring myself to feel that was part of his original thinking, but there it is.

Now having said that, I believe Satan used an animal and therefore could make the animal do what he wanted. He could express himself perfectly through that. I just underline the possibility that supernatural powers can possess any part of God's creation and we need to be aware of this and be on our guard. Now let us get down to it. Why, then, did he go for the woman? By the way, before I go to that, can I just point out, that it means

CREATION

evil is personal, not a thing but he, highly intelligent, and the Scripture says he can beat you in arguments any day. We will see how he completely twisted Eve in her thinking with less than 50 words. And examining it will take me about 25 minutes to explain what he was saying and I could spend hours just showing you how he was getting hold of her with simple words.

So here he is, intelligent, subtle, brilliant – his brain is far better than mine, able to get at me through any part of God's creation, a frightening thought. Unless you hold on to the fact that he that is in us is greater than he that is in the world. The only safety you have got. Don't you ever tackle Satan on your own. You are an absolute idiot if you do. You can see how he gets hold of people here. The New Testament says we are not ignorant of his devices. Well, if you want to know what his devices are, read about them in Genesis 3. There are two parts of the Bible I have found that Satan hates so much that he cannot bear people to study them. Genesis 3 is one and Revelation 19 is the other. And do you know, in my audio tapes we have had electronic interference, voices superimposed on mine shouting in foreign languages, blotting out what I have said about Satan on my tapes. And we have had complaints coming back from people asking "What's wrong with this tape?" And it is always when I am exposing Satan, and therefore we should just pray for protection. We are in a real situation. We are not talking about academic subjects now. He is going to hate this chapter. He hates that I am exposing his devices. I am showing you how he will get hold of you and he does not like that and he could get at me or you – through any part of God's creation.

Now, why did he go for the woman? There are three possible reasons. The first possible reason is that she did not get God's word firsthand; she got it through Adam her husband. And Satan may have hoped that because she got it second-hand, he might be able to twist it. Because his device was to *misinterpret* God's word. Satan is a great Bible commentator. He knows his

Chapter 4: Satan exposed

Bible thoroughly; he keeps quoting it. And his favourite role is interpreter of the Scripture. That is why he is so subtle because you are listening to somebody interpreting the Scripture not realising that Satan is doing it. You think anybody giving a Bible study is bound to be doing something good. But I just tell you, you need to be checking all the time to see whether these things are so. Satan loves to comment on God's Word. So maybe he went after Eve for that. I do not think that is the reason, actually.

A second reason, which is part of the answer, and I have just got to be very honest here, the New Testament does call the ladies the "weaker partner" and it is one of the reasons why God has ordered us in the way he has that those weaknesses might be covered. And there *are* some weaknesses there that Satan can exploit. He can twist a woman's thinking; he can confuse her emotions; he can seduce her will if she is on her own. That is how we are made. And it is that that lies behind Paul's teaching on women wearing hats. He is not trying to inculcate a social practice. And I have seen women with Easter bonnets in church who were nowhere near Paul's teaching. The principle of Paul's teaching is it is for the sake of the supernatural powers that she needs to be covered by a man.

You look at the number of cults that have been started by women, from Mary Baker Eddy to Madame Blavatsky, Alice Bailey. And in every case, you will find that they were not covered by a man who was their head. Now, this has profound implications. Look how many spiritist mediums are women. I am touching deep issues here. I even question whether it is right to try and get a wife converted without her husband. I question the problems that are being caused by getting hold of wives in coffee mornings and getting them ahead of their husbands spiritually. You would never get away with that with a Jewish family. You would have to go to the man if you wanted his wife. And I am saying very important things here that come right out of Genesis. Satan is looking around for uncovered women. It means that a

CREATION

church has to be very careful about covering all its single women with men. There are all kinds of implications here. Satan knows what he is doing and we ignore Scripture at our peril in this. But I don't think that is the main reason.

The main reason I believe is that Satan was trying to upset God's order and trying to get the woman to lead the man and he knew that since that was not God's order, he would be able to get in like that. Because when life is ordered God's way he cannot get in and so he quite deliberately reversed it and went after the wrong person because to him that would be the right person. And I think we have got to hear the word "ominous". No wonder God has a special concern for defenceless women. That is why widows are very near God's heart because there is no man to cover them. I shall move on.

Now let us see how Satan does it, and he only needs to talk. He does it entirely by words. God created the world by words. Satan does most of what he does by words. He is the spirit of discussion. He is the spirit of dialogue. He is the spirit of debate. He loves to start questions, just loves it. And so, he does not start with a blatant "Eve, I'm going to get you to disobey your God. Eve, I'm going to make you an atheist." He does not; he says, "Now Eve, this morning we're going to have a discussion about God," you know? And oh, it sounds so nice. There is an awful lot of dialogue going on right now but Satan just loves it. He is rubbing his hands. He loves discussion. He loves to put the right questions in and then see what happens. That is his technique. And I will tell you why – because these are his devices and I expose him now. His first step is to get you to doubt with your mind. His second step is to get you to desire with your heart and his third step is to get you to disobey with your will. And that is the way he gets in to you. And he will first cause you to cast suspicion on the Word of God until you wonder if God really *is* like that. And when he has got that distrust in your mind, then he leaves the poison to spread through your whole system and

Chapter 4: Satan exposed

it won't be long before you are wanting the forbidden thing and desire takes over from doubt. And when you have doubted in your mind and desired in your heart, frankly you just cannot resist disobeying with your will because your defences are all down now. And it is what you have set your mind and heart on that determines what your will does, did you know that?

It is what you think about and have feelings about that will determine what you do – every time. So, Satan does not go after your will; he goes after your mind first until you have got questions where you should not have. And then he goes after your heart and in particular, when he is going after your heart, he will use your eyes, the one part of the body he loves to use. Because he knows that what you look on you usually want. It is called "the lust of the eyes" in the New Testament. Most coveting comes through the eyes, did you know that?

I once preached to a large congregation half of which dogs, mostly Labradors. It was a unique experience. It was the annual meeting of the Torch Trust for the Blind and I was invited to preach and these dogs sat up and paid such attention to me because I was the only one moving or speaking and they all fixed their eyes on me. It was quite difficult to concentrate on those who could not see me. Do you know what I preached on that night? I preached on "It's better for you to lose an eye than go to hell with your sight." And I said, "Those of you who've lost your sight, will you please pity those of us who can still see? Most of our problems come through what we look at. Will you pray for us with the extra load there is on sighted people?"

And you know, it was the first time they had ever thought of it. There was one dear lady sitting there. She was 84. And she had been bitter all her life. She was not a Christian. She had been so bitter that she could not see that she had been twisted and bitter about it and of course, God could not get in. But she wrote to me... or somebody told me about her afterwards and she said, "That's the first time I've pitied sighted people." And

CREATION

her attitude changed and her bitterness went. She went home on the bus to Yorkshire with a radiant face and died four days later. But she went to heaven – with her sight. The first person she saw was Jesus.

But we are not ignorant of his devices. I am spelling them out for you so you know how he will get at you. And he is hating it.

Well now, look at the first phase, the first question. Let us see how he got hold of her mind and got it doubting. Do not look at *what* he said but look at *how* he said it. Try and hear his tone of voice and look at why he said it. He is a master of innuendo. Do you know what I mean by innuendo or insinuation? He says something and he means something else, you know? He is suggesting something. He is not saying it, just suggesting it. And it is what he is just suggesting that lodges. Do you know, that is what happens with gossip, have you ever noticed? There are many people who would not dare come right out and say, she's this and he's that, but they just kind of say, "She may have that nice house but some of us know things." Do you know what I mean?

Now, innuendo is of the Devil. Jesus said, "Let your yes be yes and your no, no." Let people know what you are saying. Innuendo is out; it is the Devil's own work to suggest, just to suggest. Look what he suggests – he says, "I hear you're not supposed to eat any of the fruit on these trees around here? God's told you not to eat any of this lovely fruit, has he?" What a subtle question. Do you know what he is doing? Accentuating the negative. He is saying, it's pretty miserable living with God, isn't it? You can't do a thing, can you? Surrounded by "thou shalt nots", miserable. He's a funny kind of God who's always forbidding you to do things, isn't he? Do you know, he gets hold of young people like this, and they get persuaded that they are so miserable at home because they can't do this and they can't do that and it is all negatives and it is all prohibition; and he gets their attention off all the things that they can do. And he nearly got Eve's attention off all the fruit that she could eat by just

Chapter 4: Satan exposed

emphasising this negative side. The Devil loves to tell you that God is a God who is always going to spoil your fun.

A boy at school was asked by his teacher, "What's your name?" And he said, "Johnny Don't." And the teacher said, "that can't be your name." "Well," he said, "that's what Mummy always calls me. 'Johnny, Don't! Johnny, Don't!'" And he thought it was his name. And he got this impression that he lived in a world that was negative, negative, negative. I remember a man saying to me, "Oh, you won't get me near church." He said, "If you knew what Sunday was like when I was a boy, oh," he said, "it was miserable. I couldn't ride my bike and I couldn't go swimming;" "oh, he said, "Sunday was terrible." I said, "Now just hold on a minute. Did you ever go for walks with your friends on Sunday?" "Yes," he said, "yes it was good fun there." I said... I knew the kind of background...I said, "Did you have singing in the evening at home?" "Yeah," he said, "I quite liked that." And I began to explore and there were a whole lot of positives in his Sunday as a boy that he had clean forgotten about – because the Devil had persuaded him that he couldn't do a thing. Do you know what I mean?

It is an insinuation. It is saying that God is a killjoy, he's a spoilsport; he doesn't want you to have any fun. He's just waiting for you and then he's going to say, "Johnny, don't." And he's a big policeman who just stops you doing what you want to do. It is a libel on God. But he does not say it outright, does h? He just kind of suggests it. Has God told you not to touch any of this fruit, then? Now, there are three things you can do with God's Word to damage it. You can add something to it, you can take something from it or you can change it. And the Devil did all three here, and Eve joined in. And she tried to defend God and she said, well, it's not *quite* like that. We *can* eat quite a lot; it's that one in the middle – and she started looking at it, you know. It's that one we can't eat. And having sort of said we can eat the rest, she is looking at one, and the rest of the discussion is

CREATION

all about that one. Oh, if Satan can get you fixed on something you cannot do and forget the things you can do, he has got you.

And she said that in fact he had told them that if they touched that one then they would die. Now God had never said that. He had said if you eat it, but she is already accentuating the negative with Satan. She is talking his language now. She said, you can't even touch it, and God never said that. He said, don't eat it. But you see she is already twisting Scripture like he did. And you will find that the pair of them between them added to God's Word, took away from God's Word and changed God's Word. And by the time you have done all those three things, you have not got much of the original meaning left. And You listen carefully to so-called Bible teachers and if you find them adding, taking away or changing, you know that Satan is getting a hold. It is those who take it just as it is and spell it out that you have got to listen to.

Now let us go a little further; that was his question. Do you notice, by the way, that he refused to use God's name? He said, let's have a discussion about God and already Adam and Eve knew that he was the LORD God – or as I told you in the last chapter, the name which is translated or just changed for Lord in capital letters in your Bible is the name, I Am, or the God Who Is, the God Who Really Is. It means the God as he is, that is his name. He says, I'm the God I Am and don't you twist anything, there's only one God and it's the one *I* am. Are you getting it? No wonder Satan would not use that name because he wants to plant a different concept of God. He does not go for atheism; he goes for bad theology. He does not try to stop you believing in God; he tries to get you believing in a different sort of God – much more subtle, much cleverer. Because, who wants to be an atheist? Very, very few. Why, a man said, "I'm an atheist, thank God!" And do you know, I was having a debate in Guildford at the university with an atheist professor of education. He was Jewish but he was an atheist and openly so, and we had a debate and boy, it was packed with students. All the communists were there. It

Chapter 4: Satan exposed

was a tremendous time. And he got on first and this was his last sentence so he said, "I am a humanist. I believe man must solve all his own problems and if he doesn't then God help us." And do you know, the whole place collapsed and they laughed and they cheered and he said, "What have I said? What have I said?" And I am afraid I just got up and I said, "Well, my text is 'God help us.'" And I just went on from there. You know, atheists are always letting themselves down because the middle part of the word *atheist* means God, did you know that? A-Theos. An atheist wrote up on a blackboard for his sermon, "God is nowhere." And he said, "Now read that to me." And the little boy read, "God is now here." He could not manage big words.

No, seriously, the Devil does not try to persuade you to be an atheist. What he does is give you a sentimental, mushy picture of God that is not the God Who Really Is. That is how he does it. He just waters it down so you think, "Oh well, God wouldn't do that." And you see, now that Satan realises Eve is already talking his language, already thinking his thoughts, already dwelling on the negative, already thinking that God is a bit of a spoilsport, he now changes questions to assertions, and he goes in pretty strongly. He said, You don't *really* think God would actually kill you for touching that? Oh, come off it now, look God is a good person. He's given you all these lovely trees. He's kind. Do you know that Satan has persuaded the vast majority of people in your town that God is not the kind of God who would ever send anyone to hell. He has. He has persuaded them and so they are perfectly happy to read all sorts of sensational Sunday paper articles about lights at the end of tunnels that people have seen in the middle of operations. You know the kind of thing? And it was all sweetness and light and they were floating and looking down on their body? Boy, if anything is of the Devil that sort of stuff is – not a word of judgment in it. Have you noticed? The Bible says it is appointed to a man once to die and after that the judgment. But all these stories of experiences like that, not a

CREATION

word of judgment. No spiritist medium ever mentions the Day of Judgment. It is all gardens and cigars and the rest of it.

And Satan says that God isn't like that. He wouldn't really punish you. He's just not that kind of a God. And I tell you that is the reason why the majority of preachers in this country never preach on hell because they do not really believe in it. Satan has kidded them that God is too kind to send anyone to everlasting punishment. But I want to tell you this: the only person who told us about hell was Jesus himself. God would not entrust such a terrible truth to anybody other than Jesus who *is* the Truth. And every bit of knowledge I have about hell came direct from the lips of Jesus. And Satan has persuaded the majority of *Christians* in this country that God is too kind to do that, and it is a lie! God is a holy God and he wants to bless us and bless us – but not on immoral conditions. So, Satan says that God isn't really like that. And immediately he realises that the questions would arise in Eve's mind, then why did he forbid that? What was his motivation? What was behind it? And so, Satan, lest she asks, rushes in with an explanation. He says that actually he's a bit scared of you. He's afraid you're going to be a rival. He's really quite a jealous person, he wants to keep his authority to himself and he knows perfectly well that if you get the kind of experience that tree will give you, you could become God. You could take over. You could live without him. You could be like he is. You could be the landlord of earth, not the tenant. I'm offering you autonomy, independence.

Do you know, that again is how he gets hold of young people again and again. Because they say, "Oh, living at home you can't do a thing"; or "Going to church you can't do a thing, you're always being told what you mustn't do, so I'm going to have my independence. going to have my autonomy; I'm going to decide what's good and bad for me. I'm going to experience good and evil for myself and find out if it's really like that." It is the same old story, and there is a very subtle appeal. Not only does Satan

Chapter 4: Satan exposed

suggest you *would* be like God but he also suggests you *could* be. You are not just a human being; you could be divine. Do you know, the philosopher Nietzsche who gave Hitler all his ideas, said this, "if gods do exist then how could I bear not to be one of them? If gods do exist, how could I bear not to be one of them?" And there is in the human heart a desire to be god of your own life, to be your own boss, to be in charge of your own business, to be the lord. Not somebody under anybody else, not a servant, but to be the boss.

There is something in all of us. It comes supremely out in Jewish nature, you know. They say that if two Jews were on a desert island there would be three synagogues built, one for him and one for him, and another that neither would be seen dead in. It is a cynical thing. They say two Jews, three opinions. But the Jewish people, when they rebelled against God became one of the most independent peoples in the world and each man wants his own business; wants to be boss; wants to run his own life. And even if he loses rather than profits, okay. He is at least his own boss. There is something in all of us that wants that independence, that autonomy, and Satan just slips it in. You could be like God and you could make your own decisions as to whether this was good for you or bad for you. How about that?

Now you see what he is doing. He is moving from doubt in the mind to desire in the heart. He is touching pride and greed, and then he just sits back and says, now watch this. And he does not say another thing. He has spoken 50 words. I have just given them very briefly to you as to what he was hinting. But he just now waits and he watches Eve and she keeps looking at that tree and she wants it. And her eyes are captured. "The eye is the lamp of the body," said Jesus. Now, we usually think that that means what is inside shines out, and it does. If you are happy or sad it comes out of your eyes; if you are tired or whatever. But he means the eye is the lamp to the inside and what comes in through there determines whether your body is full of light or darkness. And therefore, if you have got an evil eye, the whole body will be in darkness. And Eve had got the evil eye now.

It is interesting that a lot of superstition centres on the evil eye. Have you noticed? But the evil eye is the one that is right here. And Eve looked at that tree and she said, "That looks good, I bet it tastes good. And really, if it gives independence, I'd like it." And she took it and she ate it. Satan hadn't to do another thing. She did it all herself. She even picked it. And if you ever see pictures of Satan offering them an apple, just forget it. He didn't need to. And he doesn't need to do the dirty work. He just leaves you to get yourself in the mess.

And then she took it to her husband. I do not know if she gave him Satan's arguments but he just took it and he ate it. He did not even put up a fight. If Eve fell first, Adam fell worst. Now, I was speculating, why did she drag Adam into it? And I thought there were only two possible reasons. And I considered first it was because she felt good. She felt a liberated woman and she wanted him to enjoy the experience too. And I thought, is that why she rushed to him and said, "Hey, try this"? And then I thought, no, I think it might be because she felt bad. And it suddenly struck me that when we feel bad, we want to drag everybody else down to our level. We need an accomplice because sin makes us very lonely and what comforts us is to be able to say, "Well, I'm no worse than anybody else, we're all in it."

I have seen it happen in initiation ceremonies for the apprentice on the factory floor. And what is it? You know, when men are all feeling low, they drag everybody down to their level so it comforts them. There is a loneliness of sin and you are so lonely you want accomplices and if you can get a gang around you, if you can get someone else into the same mess, it really helps you, doesn't it? Because it has got them down to your level. And I believe Eve was in need of an accomplice. She was desperately lonely. She had taken it and she was feeling bad, and she thought, "My husband, I must have him in this too. I need

Chapter 4: Satan exposed

an accomplice." Does that make sense to you? Because you see it happening all around. People who have become evil have to seduce others and corrupt others in it. They cannot keep it to themselves, they have got to spread it to try and comfort their own conscience and be able to say, "Oh well everybody's like me and it's not really bad." Well, that is what she said.

Well, after they had both eaten, their eyes were opened and Satan's lie was half true. Have you ever noticed that Satan does not deal with lies, he deals with half-truths? There is enough of the truth in it to stick. they saw each other, and you know what had happened? They were no longer one flesh; they were two fleshes and they were embarrassed. Hitherto they had looked on each other's bodies and just seen the other half of their own. Now they saw something a bit different. Now they felt there is something of me I want to hide from you – that is what sin does to every marriage. It takes two who have become one and it makes them two again.

And that is one of the things the Devil is after in marriage. If he can get sin in, he will make people two again and God's order is broken. There is something that has got to be hidden, there is something that is embarrassing to share. And so you pull your fig leaves over it. Have you ever seen fig leaves? They are the silliest things to try and make clothes out of. A bit like a sycamore leaf or an overgrown oak leaf, and can you imagine sewing those together and getting yourself covered up? It would be full of holes and it was. And God said that he had to do something about it later but here they were desperately trying to cover themselves up from each other. They had never hidden anything from each other but now they see each other differently. And you know, when you see people through the eyes of sin you see them with suspicion and you wonder if they will exploit your vulnerability and your exposed nakedness. And you cannot afford to be transparent any more. This makes sense, doesn't it? It has happened to all of us in our married life because there is no a perfect marriage. There

CREATION

is no marriage that Satan has not touched in some way. And you know it happens. And the excuses, the cover-ups, the fig leaves we grab. It is pathetic because it is full of holes. Always it is full of holes, but since you are both trying to cover yourself full of holes, it just ends up in one big embarrassment.

This was even before God came into the picture. Their eyes were open, they saw things differently – but they did not see things like God saw them. They saw good and evil now, yes! But the difference was that they were not like God because God sees good from the inside and evil from the outside. But now they saw evil from the inside and good from the outside. Do you follow me in that? A good person can see evil from the outside and know about both but a bad person can only see goodness from the outside. Do you follow me? One is firsthand knowledge; one is second-hand knowledge. And as I said previous chapter, when you have lost your innocence, you cannot ever see chastity or purity from the inside again. You see it from the outside now.

And that is why Paul, writing to some Christians, says that he wants them to be babies in evil, innocent, not to know it from the inside. Okay, you cannot walk through this world without knowing it from the outside. You just could not. But that is not what we are talking about here. God knows evil from the outside, but he has never known it from the inside. He has never known what it is to lie, never! But there is not a person reading this who doesn't know lying from the inside. Because you learned how to do it when you were small. You learned to say no before you learned to say yes and so I am afraid that none of us knows goodness from the inside like God does and none of us knows evil from the outside like God does. So, we are *like* God – we know good and evil; but we are *not* and Satan promised it and it did not happen and I am afraid he has got you when he has got you there.

Well now, that is the first half of the chapter.

If you took all the people on Sunday during the sermons in

Chapter 4: Satan exposed

church in Britain and laid them end to end in one straight line head to toe they would all be very much more comfortable. I shall try and tackle the second half of the chapter more quickly. It was the first half I wanted to expand on because I want you to know how Satan operates. Have you recognised very clearly how Satan operates from your own experience as I have explained it? I mean, has this clicked with you? It really is frightening, isn't it? Or it would be if it were not for God.

Now let us see what happens in the second half of the chapter as God comes back into the picture and the serpent takes a back seat. If we do wrong, we have to face two things, the consequences and the penalty and these are two different things. If I steal some apples out of someone's garden and eat them behind the wall, I am likely to suffer the consequences of tummy ache but the penalty would be a spanking. Now, do you discern the difference? Consequences happen automatically, the penalty is personally added and applied. It is very important to understand that forgiveness does not remove the consequences of sin but it removes the penalty. We need to talk very bluntly here because you may have done things in sin, the consequences of which you will suffer the rest of your life. The penalty can be removed by forgiveness, but not the consequences. When the prodigal son came home, he had spent all his money and the consequence was he never got it back because all the father's money belonged to the other brother now. But the penalty of losing his father's relationship, that was forgiven.

And so, when God forgives, he does not remove all the consequences. If you are badly in debt being forgiven does not wipe out your debt – that is a consequence of what you have done. And if you got married before you became a Christian, being forgiven does not set you free from that marriage and suddenly give you a blank cheque to go and marry someone else. That is a consequence of your previous life but the penalty of it, that is removed. But the penalty is also added. The consequence of their

CREATION

sin was that they were ashamed, afraid, guilty, separated. But that was not the penalty because the trial had yet to take place and when God came into the garden, he started asking questions. God started in the same way as Satan started, with questions. And I used to think that God must have been ignorant or absent when he said, "Adam, where are you?" Until I realised that these questions are judicial questions and not existential questions. Now fancy me saying a thing like that.

Let me explain it. In a court case, the lawyers will get up and cross-question the witnesses. Now, the lawyer may know perfectly well what the answer is going to be but he has got to draw it out at the trial – do you follow me? He knows, but he is asking the question to get it out so that justice may be done and seen to be done. So, when God said, "Adam where have you got yourself to?" it is not that God does not know perfectly well that Adam is in the bushes with Eve – and he is not even in the same bush as she is because they are hiding from each other as well as him. And when God asks where are you, we must not think he is ignorant or has been absent. No, God is saying, Adam, where have you got yourself to, tell me. He is giving them a chance to confess and the course of world history might have been different if Adam could have brought himself to say one little word – sorry. But it is the hardest word to get out. Have you noticed that it sticks there? It is a very tough word to say. Sorry. We are so good at justifying ourselves and what we do is to try and declare that we were in the right. That is what *justify* means. We try and justify what we have done by saying, it really wasn't my fault. It's not my responsibility.

Now look what Adam, Eve and the serpent all did. They all passed the buck or the blame. And Adam said, "Well Lord, it's all the fault of that woman you sent along." Who is insinuating things now? But the key word in there is "you". Lord, if you'd never given me her it wouldn't have happened. Now that is not how he talked when she appeared, you know. He said, "This is

Chapter 4: Satan exposed

it!" But now he is saying, now if you hadn't thought that one up... And he is not only trying to blame the woman, he is trying to blame God. But that is inherent; human nature is always trying to blame the Creator, have you noticed? Human nature is always trying to blame God for the wars that happen, saying, "Why did he let it happen?" as if it was *his* fault, that *he* told people to go to war. The whole Bible is based on the two ideas of responsibility and retribution. Praise God he added a third idea – redemption. But he only *adds* it to the other two; he does not cancel out the other two when he adds that one in. It is his way of dealing with the situation, and it never avoids the principles of responsibility and retribution, otherwise the cross makes no sense at all.

There was no need for Jesus to die if God's sole aim was to reform us. Somebody had to suffer what we deserved before God could redeem, so that if you do not accept responsibility and retribution, you will not make any sense whatever of the death of Jesus on the cross. You will just see it as a sad assassination of a good man – like Martin Luther King – and that is all. But the cross grows out of what we are talking about right now. That is why it is read among the Christmas carols. Now listen to the sentences on all three. This is the God Who Really Is and the God Who Really Is is a God who curses as well as blesses. Don't you ever get the idea he only blesses. And in fact, the word for curse in Scripture is *woe, woe*. Now that word does not mean much to us except when a parent points at a child and says, "Woe betide you if you..." Have you heard that said? Well now, God says, "Woe betide you," and that is his curse. And you will find that Jesus said woe as many times as he said blessed. But I will guarantee you have heard sermon after sermon on the blesseds, on the Beatitudes – on "the beautiful attitudes" as Billy Graham calls them – and you have hardly heard any sermons on the woes, right? You have heard sermons on "blessed are the poor" but Jesus immediately added but "woe to you rich". "Blessed are those who mourn", you have heard sermons on that, but have

CREATION

you heard sermons on the next verse, "woe to you who laugh"? Now, the woes are not very popular. He talked about woe to you if you like to dress up in robes in church. I wish half the clergy in Britain could hear that woe. But it is never preached on. Woe to you if you like the chief seat in the synagogue, woe! And when God says woe, there is a curse. Now I am afraid he curses in this chapter and it is so full of emotion that he actually puts it into poetry. I told you that when God goes into poetry, it is his heart speaking. And sometimes his heart is speaking with great tenderness and it is a love poem. Other times he is speaking a curse but he does it in poetry because he is doing it with deep, deep emotion. And the first curse is on the serpent and he curses that serpent and he says, you are going to be lower than the animals from now on. And also, I'm going to put such a hostility between human beings and you that will last for the rest of history until one day you will receive a death blow from a human being. Now he is speaking to both the serpent and Satan – they are together in this. And as I have said, the result is that every descendent of that animal has got vestigial limbs.

Now, that does not mean that Satan is in every snake now but every animal descended from that original bears the marks of that original curse, just as every donkey has a cross on its back, the animal that Jesus used to ride in on Palm Sunday. It almost seems as if God leaves marks on nature for what happened at some point to remind us. That is why he put a rainbow in the sky, to remind us. He uses nature like this. But to Satan he says, this hostility between the woman and you will last until one male descendent of hers will put his foot on your head and crush your skull while you're trying to strike at his heel. That is the most amazing verse in Genesis 3, isn't it? That one day, from that woman – within her genes already – there was a male seed. He did not say from Adam, but from the woman, and at Christmas time, a woman had a male seed who 33 years later said, now is the prince of this world dealt with.

Chapter 4: Satan exposed

Satan struck at his heel but Jesus put his foot on Satan's skull and it was all promised in the curse of Satan at the beginning. I even see something more than this. Jesus said, your male seed woman, and yours, serpent, will ultimately confront each other, and I see Christ and Antichrist in that. That will be Satan's last desperate throw to make a bid for this world, to send an Antichrist, and Christ will deal with him and it will all be over. Satan hates us talking about his downfall, you know. He hates it. He is kicking.

To the woman, the curse was not menstruation. I know that that has been called the curse. I think you should be careful ladies about using that term. The curse was to do with birth and it was that your greatest joy physically would be having a man and the greatest pain and struggle you would have would be the result of it. And he said, and you'll be caught like this. You'll want that man, your desire will be for him, and yet the price of it will be that he will dominate you. And the ruling mentioned here is part of the curse, it is not part of God's order. God did not call men to be dictators and to abuse and exploit and dominate their wives but God said, that's what the Fall will do. And you can see it in house after house. And only by the grace of God can we redeem that and get it right again. That is the curse. You see how it puts that woman in tension?

And what about the man? For you, in the sweat of your brow you'll make a living. You'll want to work and yet you won't want to. It will be hard, hard. It will be a struggle. And it will almost seem as if nature is against you – thorns and thistles. Have you ever seen the thorns and thistles in the Middle East? You have not seen thorns or thistles until you have been there and seen thorns on hedges that are perhaps two or three inches long. Have you seen crowns of thorns made of those? Great big thorns. And the thistles, 6, 8, 10 feet high growing so thick that a sheep can get caught in them. You have not seen thorns and thistles until you have been out there. And you are going to have to deal with

CREATION

those. Isn't gardening one constant battle against weeds?

We are pretty comfortable here, you know, but the curse is that the whole human race will struggle to get enough food to survive. It will seem as if nature won't co-operate and that has been our life. And then he said, Adam, and you're not going to stay in this garden where you just pluck the fruit off the trees. No, you're going to have to work for your living now. You go right back to that very same plot of land and you struggle with that until you sink into it and you go right back to where you came from. And that literally happened.

I remember standing at Winston Churchill's grave in the little village of Bladon and I remember thinking, just below that stone there is a rotting, rotten stinking corpse of a little boy who used to run around this path and who was brought to this church to be christened. He is right back where he started, dust to dust. Life is a roundabout and you get off where you got on and you have lost your money. That is the curse. It is a terrible picture, this, but God was dealing with the whole situation. He had to because he is a moral God. He had told them he would. And God – unlike Satan's idea – God meant what he said. And he *does mean* what he says, and you are an absolute fool if you do not take seriously what God says to you. And anybody who tries to add to this Word or take from it or change it will find out how mistaken he has been when he realises that God never says anything that he does not mean. And they found out the hard way.

Now, that might be the end of the story and it would be a pretty sad end. Think of the new words that have come into Genesis 3 that were not there in Genesis 2 or in Genesis 1. Here is the list of new words: pain, fear, sorrow, death – what a vocabulary. And none of those words need have been in our language. They are the language of sin; they are the vocabulary of disobedience. And they need never have been.

Let us just close by looking at what Adam did and what God did. Adam realised something extraordinary in the curse. I do not

Chapter 4: Satan exposed

think it had dawned on him that he and Eve were going to have children and I told you that sex was primarily for partnership and they were just husband and wife together and enjoying each other. But when God cursed Eve with pain of childbearing Adam must have thought, we're going to be like the animals; we're going to have kids. Eve, do you realise you're going to be the mother of all living human beings? So he called her Eve, which means life-giving or lively, and he gave her that name but exercised his rule over her in doing so. But I reckon that even in the curse he heard something that he responded to. But look what God did. God said, get those fig leaves off and killed some animals, the first time that animals had been slaughtered in history, other than natural death. And God killed some animals and he brought some fur coats for both of them, and he said, now get these on.

Even as he judged them, even as he sentenced them to death, even as he cursed them, there is something in God that says, I can't bear to see you like this. "In wrath, remember mercy." And God is saying that he can only cover you properly when the life of innocent blood has been taken — that is his principle. And that was the only way he could bring home seriously to them that if they were going to cover guilt and shame it had got to be taken so seriously that the sacrifice of innocent life must have taken place. And all that leads straight through to the cross, doesn't it? But then God said, but the one thing I can't do is let you stay around forever, not now. If I let you live forever, you'd spoil my universe forever, and so God ordered them to get out of this garden. I can't let you touch that other tree now, the tree that I put there to keep you alive, the tree that would minister eternal life to you, I can't let you have that now. And he kicked them out and put angels with flaming swords there to keep them out of the way.

And Eden has disappeared because you see God planted it as a park and it needed tilling and cultivating. It needed looking after and he put Adam in it to look after it, but without Adam to look after it, well, it just reverted to nature, it reverted to the state of all the rest of the earth, and it has now gone and you can't find it. You can search that whole area of Armenia and you just cannot find any trace. The two trees have gone, the park has gone. It was planted out. You would have recognised it as that but it is now the same as everywhere else, it has reverted to the natural and it has gone. And Eden is no more – Paradise has been lost.

Now in conclusion, let me say this final thing. How does all this affect the rest of us? There is a Jewish answer and a Christian answer and they're quite different. The Jewish rabbi will tell you this – Adam is every man; this is not historical truth, this is existential truth, this is psychological truth. It is a story with a moral to it. It did not actually happen but it is what happens to us. Now that is the official Jewish line and a great philosopher called Martin Buber is one of the Jews who first taught us to think of it as a kind of existential myth. And therefore, they say that this is the story of every man and woman's life. We come into life as an innocent baby and we are faced with a choice and we can either go the right way or the wrong way and it is our choice and we are free to make it and if you make the right choice, you will be a good man and if you make the wrong choice, you will be a bad man, but it is up to you.

Now that is Jewish teaching and it sounds very convincing and a lot of Christian preachers take that line with Genesis 3 as well and they treat it as a myth but that is full of truth about each of us. And certainly, I can identify with a lot in the chapter. There is one thing I cannot identify with: that they started innocent. And that is not true of me and it is not true of you.

And the *Christian* interpretation of this story in the New Testament is that Genesis 3 never happened again because that was the beginning and there has not been another beginning. And even in the Old Testament there are hints. King David, when he sinned and he killed Bathsheba's husband or got him murdered and then took Bathsheba in. That was a terrible thing to do. He

Chapter 4: Satan exposed

murdered, he committed adultery, he coveted, he stole, all in one act. And when he realised how wrong he had been, he said this: "In sin my mother conceived me" (Psalm 51). And he did not mean that sex is sin. He did not mean that. He said, I've been bad since the moment of my conception, and that's the truth. Jesus said to us, "If you then, *being evil*, know how to give good gifts to your children…" Being evil – that was Jesus' opinion of human nature. We are not born innocent. You may look at a nice little baby in a pram but that baby is not innocent. One parent told me, "The trouble with having babies is you see your own faults developing in them." And I am afraid I know I have passed on sin to my three children. It is a very disturbing thing to watch coming out and realise you passed it on with your genes because Adam passed it on with his genes. The truth is we are not "every man". Every man is not his own Adam. We do not start innocent and then make a choice. We are not free to make that choice. We don't start with innocence. We *all* have evil thoughts. You never have to teach a child to lie but you have to teach him to tell the truth, right? You never have to teach a child to be naughty, only to be good. You never have to teach a child to be rude, only to be courteous. You never have to teach a child to sin, only to be right. Now why is that? Why are we *all* in it now? Why is there not a single exception? Why can no man come to me and say, "I chose not to eat the fruit of that tree and I'm good?" There is not a man or woman who can say it, so what is the explanation for the fact that *none of us* has ever been able to make the right choice since then without any exception?

Well, the answer is that our destiny was in that one man and that is an unpalatable truth; I would like to feel that I have nothing to do with my great-grandfather, you see. I would like to feel that I start fresh but I do not, I do not. Some lady in Cornwall dug back our family tree to about 1465 or somewhere around there. And she found a description of someone called Pawson from the fifteenth Century there and she sent it to me. It was alarming, it really was. It described my hair, my skin, it described my temper. I am not going to go into details but it was uncanny. And I read this – that's me! I'm a Pawson. And somebody in the fifteenth Century was just like me. And all the temperamental problems I have, he had. And I got them from him. It is shattering.

An American came over to Lancashire when my wife and I lived there. He had saved up all his life to come and visit his birthplace and when he retired he spent his savings on a ticket. And he came to Manchester and he had his birth certificate and on it was the address where he was born, Number 1 Southall Street, Manchester, and he found the place – and it was Strangeways Prison and he discovered his mother had been in prison but they put that address on the birth certificate. He spent all his life savings to discover that.

Look, in Adam all men die. There is something that Adam did that he acquired and passed on in his genes and I believe the Bible says that that can be acquired and passed on in genes. I agree with the evolutionist there, or with one of the things he says. And he has passed it on and we are all in the same boat. And there is not one of us who started innocent. I am afraid we just took to eating from the tree of good and evil as naturally as a duck to water. Isn't that the truth? Just as soon as we could we tried it. Just as soon as somebody told us not to touch it, we touched it. Just as soon as somebody slaps an X certificate on it, we want to see it. Just as soon as we were told, "Johnny don't!" we did. Because one man decided our destiny.

And people say, "I resent that. Why should one man land that lot on me?" Well, you may resent it but now let me tell you another side of it which will make you glad that that happened because the destiny of the human race is in the hands of two men. There has been a second Adam. And "as in Adam all die, so in Christ shall all be made alive." And I tell you, this is the basis for the whole Bible, that into this human race came one new man with innocence who kept it the whole life through; who

Chapter 4: Satan exposed

refused to eat fruit that he had been forbidden to eat, and who brought a new man into the human race, a man who got right to the end of his life without ever having to say sorry. That is Jesus. And a second Adam to the fight and to the rescue came. And the rest of the Bible is built on that. It assumes that one man can do something for the rest of us. And if one man could get us all into that mess, one man could get us all out of it. That is the gospel!

And see what opens up now that he has come with his head in the very thorns, which were the curse, and he comes and he lives an obedient life. And he says to a dying terrorist, I'll get you into Paradise today. I'll get you back into Eden tonight. And he so opens up the possibilities that because he came, there is to be a new heaven and a new earth and the tree of life is going to be in it and we can go and eat it again. Access is opened up to the tree that will keep you alive forever. That is the good news. That is the whole drama of the Bible and if you cut Genesis 3 out of the Bible, the whole thing will collapse. It will not make sense. If you treat Genesis 3 as a fairy tale or a myth then frankly you have nothing left to build on because the rest does not make any sense. If one man did not get us all into the mess, one man cannot get us out. But one man disobeyed and lost us Paradise and one man obeyed and got it back for us. The seed of the woman bruised the serpent's head and he can prevent that serpent from touching you.

I think I have said enough but look, I am not giving you a lecture. I am not trying to entertain you or to interest you or to find some new truth or to give some novelty. I give you this message so that you might rejoice to be in Christ and out of Adam because Adam will take you to your grave, back to the dust. It is the only place he can take you, "ashes to ashes, dust to dust". But Christ said, "I came that they may have life, and may have it abundantly." He wanted us to have it eternally. That was what he came to do. And I would just think you were a fool if you turned Christ down and missed such an opportunity.

CREATION

You remain under the curse if you do, that is for sure. But when he died on the cross, it was said of him that he bore our curse on the tree. Isn't it amazing? It is one book; it was written over a period of 1,400 years by 40 different people with no editor, no co-ordinator, no committee overseeing, none of them knowing they were writing the Bible. And it is just one big story, a true drama in which God and Satan and you are the players.

CHAPTER 5:

EVOLUTION AND ITS EFFECTS

The four chapters above were largely an exposition of Scripture. This chapter will be rather more on the science side of the question in order to do justice to many of the questions I have been asked on the scientific side.

But I want to divide this chapter into two halves again. In the first half I want to talk about evolution as a physical idea – in other words as a theory of how our bodies came to be, a *physical* idea. And then in the second half I want to talk about evolution as a philosophical idea because it is the second thing that has done the most damage. It was the *philosophical* idea as it was picked up by men like Karl Marx and Adolf Hitler that actually plunged our century into such terrible wars as we have seen. And so we are going to look first at the physical idea for the actual physical side of evolution, the development of plants, animals and man. And then we are going to look at what happened to that idea when it was applied politically, in business and in many other areas and did an immense amount of damage. And in that second half I am going to tell you the inside story of what happened to Charles Darwin spiritually, of what happened to his heart and mind as a result of the ideas that he taught because that is a very relevant part of the story which most people have no idea about. And I personally would not like to be in the state *he* was when he came to die.

Well now, that gives you an outline for the chapter. I want to read two passages of Scripture. They are not *directly* on the subject but I think they will give us a few pointers later. Here

CREATION

is the first; one is from the Old Testament, one from the New. From the Old Testament:

"Oh Lord our God, the majesty and glory of your name fills all the earth and overflows the heavens. You have taught the little children to praise you perfectly. May their example shame and silence your enemies. When I look up into the night skies and see the work of your fingers, the moon and the stars you have made, I cannot understand how you can bother with mere puny man, to pay any attention to him. And yet you have made him a little lower than the angels and placed a crown of glory and honour upon his head. You have put him in charge of everything you made. Everything is put under his authority, all the sheep and the oxen and wild animals too; the birds and the fish and all the life in the sea. O Jehovah our Lord, the majesty and glory of your name fills the whole earth."

That is one view of man, which is the right view. Now, the passage from the New Testament is this:

"For the truth about God is known by men instinctively. God has put this knowledge in their hearts. Since earliest times men have been able to see the earth and the sky and all that God made and have known of his existence and great power so they will have no excuse. Yes, they knew about him alright but they wouldn't admit it or worship him or even thank him for all his daily care. And after a while they began to think up silly ideas of what God was like and what he wanted them to do. The result was that their foolish minds became dark and confused. Claiming themselves to be wise without God they became utter fools instead and then, instead of worshipping the glorious ever-living God, they took wood and stone and made idols for themselves, carving them to look like mere birds and animals and snakes and men. So God let them go ahead into every kind of sexual perversion and do whatever they wanted to. Yes, vile and sinful things with each other's bodies. Instead of believing what they knew was the truth about God, they deliberately chose to

Chapter 5: Evolution and its effects

believe lies so they prayed to the things God made but wouldn't obey the blessed God who made these things"....

"So it was that when they gave God up and would not even acknowledge him, God gave them up to do everything their evil minds could think of. Their lives became full of every kind of wickedness and sin, of greed and hate, envy, murder, fighting, lying, bitterness, gossip. They were back-biters, haters of God, insolent, proud braggarts, always thinking of new ways of sinning and continually being disobedient to their parents. They deliberately misunderstood, broke their promises and were heartless and without pity. They were fully aware of God's death penalty for these crimes yet they went right ahead and did them anyway and encouraged others to do them too."

The reason I have read that second passage is this: The choice between creation and evolution is not just a mental choice. It is a *moral* choice. It is not just a matter of mind; it is a matter of heart and will. And I want to show you that the reason why the idea of evolution caught on so readily was that people desperately *wanted* to believe it. And the reason why they wanted to believe it was that it would set them free from God. And Charles Darwin's own life illustrates that perfectly. That was why he taught it – because he was on the run from God and he wanted to live without God. That was why he took a ship called HMS Beagle and went off to South America. He was a Jonah.

Now let us look at the physical idea of evolution and then the philosophical idea. Ever since man has been conscious of his own mind, he has asked questions and the basic question has been how did I get here? And there have been many answers to that question. But one of the oldest is the answer of evolution. It is not a new idea. You can trace it way back to ancient Greece. Aristotle believed in evolution, which raises the funny question, how come, then, that Charles Darwin got all the publicity? I mean, even his own grandfather, Erasmus Darwin, was a believer in evolution. That was where Charles got it from, from his granddad. But nobody talks about his granddad. At exactly the same time as Charles Darwin was on a boat touring the West Indies, there was another man called Wallace who was on a boat touring the East Indies. And Wallace came to the same conclusion as Charles Darwin at exactly the same moment. And yet no one had heard of Wallace until a programme on TV entitled The Forgotten Voyage, which was about the other man who was on a ship working out natural selection at the same time.

The thing is, Charles Darwin got his work published first and he beat Wallace to the post, just by a matter of weeks. So, everybody has heard of Charles Darwin and that raises the question, why should he get all the credit? What is so special about him when men have believed this idea from Aristotle right through? And I could give you a long history of people who believed that somehow some forms of life had changed into other forms, and that that is how the great variety we see in the world today got here. It is an old, old idea. But it was the publication in 1859 of a book called *On the Origin of Species* by Charles Darwin that actually did the trick. And the reason was that, firstly, he was the first man to give a plausible explanation of how it could have worked; not just the idea but he theorised about a possible mechanism. He was the first, not only to say I believe that's what happened, but he was the first really to say I believe this is *how* it happened. And what he said seemed very reasonable, very plausible, very credible. Furthermore, he was able to write it in such a way that for the first time, ordinary people in the street felt they could understand science. Hitherto it had been a study that was limited to the scholars who could use the right language, but he was the first "pop" scientist. Now we have a spate of them on TV, usually waving their hands about as they explain.

If Charles Darwin were alive now, he would be straight onto TV because he could put things in such a way that people would swallow them. And so here was a man who was able to say to the

Chapter 5: Evolution and its effects

man in the street, I can tell you how it happened. Now, nobody had ever done that before. They just held the idea with rather "high fallutin'" language and had never communicated it but when that book came out, it just became a best seller overnight. At first, the book only dealt with plants and animals but it was not long, only a few years, before the second book came from his pen entitled *The Descent of Man*, and that, of course, put man in the whole process as well and *that* is when the real furore began. But even within a year of the first book being published there was a debate at the British Association – that is an annual gathering of top scientists – in Oxford in 1860, and unfortunately a bishop, the Bishop of Oxford, Bishop Samuel Wilberforce no less, decided to oppose this new idea and instead of doing his homework and studying a bit of science he just laughed it out of court and made jokes about monkeys. The silliest thing Christians can do is not to meet a thing with honesty. To try to laugh it out of court is not good enough and we cannot get away with that. Nor did the good bishop. And he was proved a fool and the atheist who opposed him, a man called Huxley, Thomas Huxley – from whom Julian Huxley was descended – made mincemeat out of the bishop. And I am afraid from that moment people thought that all Christians were head-in-the-sand ostriches who would not face questions honestly.

Now, you may be dissatisfied at the end of this chapter that I have not answered all your questions because there are some questions about evolution that I cannot answer yet and I think we have got to be as honest as Jesus was, as I said. And when he did not know something, he said so and I think we have got to be equally humble and honest. But there are a number of things that we can begin to answer and I am going to.

Now let us first of all get some terminology right. We have got to use the right words. There are just five words you need to learn that I would like you to get a hold of because I am going to be using them quite a bit.

CREATION

The first two words in the theory – and that is all it is – in the theory of evolution are *variation* and *selection* and these were the two words around which Charles Darwin built his theory. They are very simple concepts. The first concept is that in any population of plants or animals you are always going to get variety. No two will be exactly the same, largely because in reproduction two people sexually combining, combine in different ways their own characteristics; so, our three children are all different from my wife and myself. This is a normal fact of life and he noticed that variation. Now, no one of us wants to quarrel with that. There are no two trees the same, no two blades of grass the same, no two people the same. There is variation right through creation. No problem with that.

The next step was when Darwin said that as these variations occurred, the ones that were most suited to their environment, the ones that were best adapted to the world, would naturally be selected and others would die out. For example, up in the northeast of England there are some moths, and I come from the northeast so I have seen these. And, incidentally, I studied science under the leading evolutionist, Professor Harrison, in this country, which was a fascinating experience. And he could show us before our very eyes, variation and selection. And these moths used to be light coloured, almost white, but over the last hundred years they have changed and they are now largely black. And the reason was that the part of the country where I come from is a coal mining country and these moths that were light showed up against the coal slag heaps so the birds could just pick them off whereas the darker ones, the birds did not spot so easily. So, all the light ones got picked off and gradually the overall population got darker and darker and darker. And now they are pretty well black. It was not that they picked up the black colour from the coal, it was that the variations of colour meant that some of them got picked off and so gradually as they went on breeding, they bred darker and darker moths. You follow me?

Chapter 5: Evolution and its effects

That is variation and selection and we saw it happening before our eyes. I have seen it.

But Darwin said that is how *everything* came to be, not just that is how light moths became dark moths, but that is how horses became dogs or dogs became horses and that is how monkeys became men and that is how everything turned into everything else – and that was his great theory.

Now, it was a theory that had one great difficulty to it and that is that the rate of this variation is so slow and so small that it would take far too long to produce all the different species we have got in the world today. Now, he struggled with that idea and he could not cope with it. But in fact, based on *his* theory we needed millions upon millions of years to produce all the species there were because variation is slow and it is small.

So, another man who came along later, a man called Lamarck, brought in a further idea which has modified Darwin's theory and his idea was *mutation*, that not only will there be small variation but from time to time there will be a huge change from inside a creature. He could not explain how it would happen but he said, somewhere there must be big changes, sudden changes, instead of these many small, little ones. And so the two theories can be pictured. Darwin thought of a steady, slow evolution with lots and lots of small little changes and the different species as it were dropping off that ascending escalator at different levels. But Lamarck saw it much more as a staircase – a little variation then a big mutation, a little variation, big mutation. And so, he was making room for bigger changes than Darwin ever thought possible.

Now, those are roughly the basic three ideas that evolutionists work with. Any scientist reading this is probably crawling with frustration at my over-simplifying but I am trying to get it at the point where we can all get hold of the terms.

The other two words I want you to learn are *micro-evolution* and *macro-evolution*. Micro means little evolution, macro means

CREATION

big, and you will understand these terms now in the light of what I have already said. Micro-evolution says that a horse that high can develop into a horse that high. Macro-evolution says that a horse can develop into an elephant. Now I am putting it again into an over-simplified way. In other words, micro-evolution, little evolution, says there can be variations within limits, within a group of creatures. Macro-evolution says the whole lot came from one. Now we are going to ask as we go through can we believe either or both of these? And my own position is this: Micro-evolution is a fact of life. I have no problem with it, nor does the Bible. For example, from Adam must have come all the black men, all the pink men the brown, all the yellow. From one man must have come this whole variety of human beings. That is micro-evolution. But that man has come from an ape is macro. And unless we think clearly of this, we fall into the trap of people who show us the evidence for micro-evolution and then argue for macro-evolution. Do you follow me?

And I think we need to go along with them on the first and stop at the second rather than dismiss the whole lot. I believe in the evolution of those moths in the Durham coalfields. It is micro-evolution. It was within limits. It did not change a moth into a spider but it did change a white moth into a black one. And I think we have got to again distinguish very clearly between big and small evolution.

Now let me just mention one of the greatest fallacies of thinking that lies behind the whole issue and then we will move into very practical matters. Supposing I was talking to you and giving a lecture on the evolution of the aeroplane. Then I could talk about micro- and macro-evolution. Micro-evolution would be the gradual change in the shape of the aeroplane wings, whether they were straight out or slightly swept back and gradually getting more swept back. You can see a gradual evolution in the design of the aeroplane in the shape of the wings. That would be what I would call micro. Macro-evolution

Chapter 5: Evolution and its effects

would be the change from gliding to powered flight, the change from piston engines to jet engines and the change from sonic to supersonic. Do you see? There are certain changes which we can say are gradual and small and others which are big and radical. Now, have I said enough? But the fallacy is this. I could show you slide after slide about the evolution of the aeroplane. I could show you the small developments and then the big changes and it *would* be like that staircase. But the fallacy would come if I said, now that proves that the Wright Brothers' plane turned into Concord over a period of years. Do you follow the fallacy? Similarity of design does not prove descent. It proves a common designer. Now that is perhaps the most important thing I want to say in this chapter.

Just the fact that you can produce a diagram of how the aeroplane evolved does not prove that it did that on its own. It does not prove that one aeroplane turned into another. It can also prove that there was one designer whose ideas changed. Now I hope you follow that; that is a key to logical thinking about evolution because most of the handbooks on evolution contain such charts – a shambling ape to an upright man walking along with a rolled umbrella at the other end of the strip cartoon. Have you seen them? And so they draw a lot of it owing to imagination. But they draw these sorts of shambling apes up to the man and it is a beautiful series. But even if they have drawn it accurately, that does not prove a thing except a common designer. I hope you follow me. It does not prove that that turned into that, that turned into that. Because you could draw aeroplanes in the same sort of line and you would see how they gradually changed. I have got some books on aeroplanes and there is such a diagram of showing how Concorde developed from a number of fighter planes before it, and it is fascinating. You can just see the shape emerging, but it proves no evolution at all in terms of spontaneous change.

Now let us look at first of all the origin of plants and animals. I find it very important when looking at this whole question to

CREATION

ask two things: What does Scripture actually say? And what has science actually discovered or proved? Because there is far too much theology and far too much theory flying around in the whole debate. I want to know what Scripture actually *says* and not what I *thought* it said. And I want to know what science has actually proved and not what it *thinks* it has proved. And when I insist on what Scripture actually says and what science actually has discovered I find that there is not nearly the conflict that I thought there was. The conflict was a theology that *thought* it understood the Bible, and a *theory* of evolution and theology and theories will always come into conflict. I believe ultimately Scripture and science *must* be reconciled. If science is honest and Scripture is true, then they must be reconciled. You cannot live in two worlds. I cannot be the kind of schizophrenic scientist who is one thing in the laboratory and another thing in church on Sunday. I have got to live in one world. This is one world because God made it and therefore what he has put into the world and what he says he has put into the world must be one and the same thing. So, I cannot rest in a dual world, a kind of schizophrenic thinking.

So, what has Scripture actually said about the plants and animals first? Well, there are only two things that Genesis actually has said. One is God said, let the earth produce vegetation and let the earth produce all living creatures; not, *I'm* going to produce them. He says, *let the earth produce those*. Now that is an incredible statement when you look at it. It is as if God handed over the job of producing plants and animals to the earth and said, get on with it, produce those things for me. Now that is quite a statement. It would make room for a very great deal of evolution among the plants and animals, would it not if God handed over that responsibility in that way? I am just pointing out what the Scripture actually says. He did not say, let *us* produce plants and animals or I'm going to. He said, let the earth get on with that; let the land produce them. So, I do not have problems

Chapter 5: Evolution and its effects

with animals and plants coming out of the earth. But on the other hand, there is another phrase in Genesis which also is part of God's Word which says, "according to their kinds", and these two phrases seem to me to have to be balanced. They seem almost to contradict one another. On the one hand it is as if God says, let the earth produce them all, get on with it, and then he says, ah, but produce them according to their kinds. So, what can we make of this second phrase? First of all, the word "kind" is not the same as the modern word "species", so let us get that out of our minds. *Kind* in Scripture means *grouping* and it is probably much larger a word than an individual species. Kind does not mean an elephant plus a giraffe plus something else. Kind in Scripture tends to mean all four-legged animals or all flying things or something – it is quite a large group. And certainly, *according to their kinds* means that they must reproduce consistently so that a pig must not produce puppies. But having said all that, I believe that we are left with those two phrases with an impression of micro-evolution but not necessarily macro.

But there is an awful lot of leeway within the language and I do not think the Scripture ties us down to the faith or the theology that God created a duck here and a hen there and a goose there, as if he sort of was a celestial Paul Daniels, that he was just producing and putting. That, I think, is not the theology that Scripture is encouraging us to believe. The Scripture is saying, let the earth produce this but let there be a consistency in what is produced so that they reproduce themselves. Now that is a combination of freedom and order. It is variation within limits and I would say the Scripture does not at this point for the plants and animals either say that all things had to come separately or that they all had to come from one. I just do not think it says anything that ties us down to one or the other. Therefore, that to me leaves room for science to find out whether in fact they came all from one or came separately or came in a *few* groups which

CREATION

then varied. It really would not affect my theology whichever science discovers about plants and animals. I am not dealing with man yet, but it would not upset my theology if science actually proved any one of these possibilities.

But what has science actually proved? The intriguing thing is that far from proving that all plants and animals came from one origin and one source of life, the fossil record seems to point in a different direction and ultimately the fossil record is the proof or disproof, I believe, of evolution. And as far as animals are concerned – and plants, but let us stay with animals – here are some facts.

First of all, most of the main animal groups appear quite quickly and suddenly. They do not come spread over a huge, long period. In one level, in the Cambrian era, they are there and they are already different from each other when they first appear. Now that is quite unusual. There is variation within the types. You can trace the changes of the horse, but the horse has always been a horse and in fact, the first staggering thing about the fossil record is that they did seem to come in groups, not from one but in groups. There they are.

Furthermore, the second startling fact about the fossil record is that you hardly ever find a half-and-half animal. There are just a few that *might* be transitional forms as they say but most of them are clearly what they are. And some of them have not changed ever since they first appeared. The common crab was exactly the same when it first appeared as it is today. It has just not changed. Many of the insects appeared millions of years ago and are exactly the same right now. There has been no change at all. So, there are some very surprising things in the fossil record about animals. Some have not changed, they all tended to appear fairly quickly and completely developed. And another surprising thing is that the simple forms of life and the complex forms of life appeared at the same time. We would have expected the very simple forms to appear here and then much, much later down the

Chapter 5: Evolution and its effects

road some of the complicated ones but that is not so.

Now, I am speaking relatively because geological periods are long, as you know. So, when I say they appeared quickly I do not mean between Tuesday and Thursday, but I do mean in one era. And so, with all these surprising things that are emerging from science, I really find no conflict at all between Scripture and science. The situation is still up for grabs; it is still wide open. And whatever they discover is not going to shake deeply my understanding of Scripture because I think God deliberately gave us the language about the creation of plants and animals in, not an ambiguous but in a less specific way than would be needed to tie us down to any particular theory as to how plants and animals came. And the two facts that God said, let *the earth* produce plants and animals according to their kinds – those two statements – not a thing that science has discovered has affected those two statements one iota. So, frankly, there is a lot of song and dance about the animals and the plants which there need not be.

The great question is not *how* did all the plants and animals come about but was it *planned*? Were they all accidents or was there a design? *That* to me is the big issue. Did he fall or was he pushed – that is the real issue. Did all these species simply fall into being or were they *pushed*? Was somebody behind it? And that of course is a question that must be answered on other grounds.

Now, secondly, with the problem of man as distinct from animals and plants, we *are* into real problems. It is here that the real difficulties arise. I do not believe they arise over plants and animals, but when we come to man, Scripture says certain things about man which are not easy to reconcile with what evolutionists say about man. So, let us look at that. look at what Scripture has actually *said* and then at what science has *actually* discovered.

What has Scripture actually said about the creation of man? Well, the first thing we noticed was that Scripture says that God created man from exactly the same material that he created the animals. That is the first thing. So that is one factor we must take

CREATION

into account. Just as the animals were made from the ground, so Adam was made from the ground, the clay, the soil, the dust – Adam in Hebrew. But all the other things that are said about man make *his* origin *different* from the plants and animals. For example, to the plants and the animals, God says let *the land* produce them but for man, he says let *us* produce him, and that is a real difference – as if man is coming from quite a different angle into the situation. Do you follow me? Not, let the land produce man but let *us* produce this one as if, we'll take the responsibility back from the earth and *we'll* do this one.

Then, of course, there is the statement that man is created – not made, created. And that word means, as I told you, something new that had not been there before. And then there is the statement that man alone is in the image of God. And then there is the statement that woman was not made from the dust but from man. She was cloned from his side. Now, all this tells me that man and woman were a *special* creation. They are not in the same category as plants and animals and it is at this point that we really run into the evolutionist who says that man *was* in that same process. Whereas to me, all that the Bible says about man says that he was *not* in the same process. He came a different way, which raises all the problems now. And we have got to face them honestly.

And I want to divide man into two groups –historic man and prehistoric man. And we will begin with historic man because there is really not much problem with historic man. I mean man as we know him, by the records he has kept of himself through history, writing his own history. And as we know, historic man, the human race today, is one race, it is not a variety of species. The human race is one; the unity of the human race is established from every conceivable angle. You can marry any human being in the world whether it is the most educated person or the most primitive Aborigine, you can marry; your chromosomes match. If you are in the right blood group you can have a blood

Chapter 5: Evolution and its effects

transfusion. Every human being alive in the world today can learn the language of every other human being, did you know that? It is not easy, but you can. And so I marvelled when I had a meal in West Berlin with an Auca Indian who was one of the Indians who had killed the missionaries in Ecuador in 1952. And here was this savage tribesman from the heart of the Amazon jungle who did not even know what a knife and fork on the table were for and yet I looked at him with his filed teeth and I would have trusted my baby to him. And we shared totally and the Spirit enabled us to understand one another's heart perfectly. It was quite an experience to meet that man in West Berlin of all places. He had just been flown in from the Amazon jungle and had never been in a plane before. And yet the way and the speed with which he adapted to West Berlin was astonishing, straight out of the Amazon jungle. And you just realise the human race is *one* species and of course that is because, as Paul says in Acts 17, of one man he made the whole race – all the nations.

So, there is no problem with historic man being biblical man, if you like. In fact, in moral experience we all have a conscience too. You will never meet a man – even a stone-age man in New Guinea – who does not have a conscience. He knows the difference between right and wrong. He may not have the same list of right and wrong as you have but he knows the difference. So, there is no problem with historic man and the Bible. There are some very interesting things coming out; for example, through agricultural archaeology.

I am an agriculturalist – or I was – and I am fascinated by farming and agriculture and it fascinates me to learn where the first domestication of animals and the first cultivation of wild grasses which became wheat and barley happened. Do you know where it happened? It happened in a place that, according to Genesis 2, would be just outside the Garden of Eden. It happened exactly where God told Adam to learn to till the ground instead of eating fruit. And the history of agriculture – right back to

CREATION

Neolithic times – goes right back to the very one spot in the world where Adam was told to get on and farm it. I find little things like this just fascinating.

But the *problem* comes with prehistoric man and we must face this very honestly. And I am going to be very honest at the beginning and say that I do not know the complete answer to this problem yet. I am going to give you some guidelines so that we can at least do some thinking about it. But I do not have the complete answer. I am sure you realise that now we have discovered more and more remains of skeletons which have all the marks of being at least man-like, and the Latin word for man is *homo* and most of these finds are now labelled *homo* whether they are *homo sapiens*, which is modern man, or *homo erectus* or *homo neanderthalensis* – Neanderthal man – or Peking man or Java man or Australia man. You have heard all these phrases and they are used so freely you must be aware of them.

Now the dating of these men is going further and further back – provided the dating is right. And we used to think in terms of a man 50,000 years old being prehistoric. How old do you think the oldest skeleton now discovered is claimed to be? I was reading up on the very latest discoveries. How old do you think they are now saying we can go back with prehistoric man? Well, the latest claim is that they have found a skeleton in Ethiopia – or parts of it – that are several million years old, so that these claims have been pouring out. At first, we thought 30,000 then 50,000 then 150,000 years ago with Neanderthal man and it went back and back and back and now the latest finds by Leakey in Tanzania and a Frenchman in Ethiopia and further south in South Africa, the latest finds they are claiming several *million* years ago. They are finding skulls that they claim to be homo – man. So, we are really faced with a problem.

So, let me just say first of all three things about their discoveries that we need to just bring into the picture and then I am going to run through the five possible explanations. The

Chapter 5: Evolution and its effects

three things that I think we need to remember are these.

First, they have not yet discovered a creature that is half ape and half man. All the things they have found are *either* apes or men. They have not discovered anything halfway. Now that is interesting. There is a huge gap still then. They have not found a lot of missing links. The link is still missing and so some of the finds in southern Africa have been clearly said to be apes and others have been clearly said to be men but in fact, there are no ape-men yet. That is the first thing I think we just need to remember and it is largely on the teeth that that identification is made. As you probably know, an ape has an oblong jaw with molars down the side then two huge sticking-out teeth here and then a little row of incisors at the front, whereas all human jaws are a semicircle with the molars going straight round into the incisors and back down again. And all the jaws that they *have* found are one or the other. So that is the first thing we need to remember.

The second thing is this. All of the scientists who have discovered these say that a number of these groups are *not* our ancestors. They appeared and became extinct and they find that very difficult to explain but they are all quite honest in saying that they do not see these groups all as our ancestors. They are claiming one or two of the groups are but many of them, they are saying they just arose and disappeared like dinosaurs; and so we do not really know how they fit in.

The third thing that I think we need to know is this. They do not follow a progressive order like all the school textbooks showed, which showed a man with a little brain getting a little bigger brain, and getting a massive brain and then finishing up like a brainy person or like any of us. Or in simple terms, the growth of brain capacity from about 400cc to about the modern 1500scc, but you have seen all the charts, haven't you? But in fact, the "early men" that they are discovering have large brains and that has really upset the large brains of those who discovered them.

CREATION

I am waiting to hear much more clearly from the scientists before I will commit myself to a final answer because *they* are confused at the moment, and honestly so. They are saying, we just don't know what is happening. Every new discovery throws overboard their theory, so I am just waiting on that one. Now let us look at the five possibilities and sooner or later, *when* more evidence comes through science, we are going to have to choose one of these five positions.

The first possibility is that scientists are completely misled. That is the first thing and some Christians delight in saying, "Well, the Piltdown Man was a fraud." How do they know it was a fraud? Because scientists said so. So, if you are going to claim the Piltdown Man as a fraud and say everything else is a fraud then you have got to say, "Well, how do I know the Piltdown Man was a fraud? And you know it might have been real but it was science who said it was unreal. So, if you are going to accept the findings of science that Piltdown was a fraud, then you ought to be fair and accept what they say is real is real. I do not think the first possibility is one. I am prepared to acknowledge that scientists are honestly trying to find out reality. I cannot dismiss all the Carbon 14 dating as rubbish. So, number 1 is not an option for *me* but it seems to be for some Christians.

The second possibility is that Scripture is false and is giving us false information and that in fact Genesis 1, 2 and 3 are a myth and therefore not historically true; they are just a fable containing some truths. Well, I am afraid I cannot accept *that* one. That is not an option for me either. I believe God would not speak to us in fables, or if he did, he would indicate they *are* fables as he does in some places in the Bible. I believe once you cut out the historical truth of the early chapters of Genesis you are in dead trouble with the whole of the rest of the Bible. So that is not an option for me, though some adopt it. *Many modernists* adopt that.

The third option is that prehistoric men are not men in the biblical sense. They were highly developed animals, almost as

Chapter 5: Evolution and its effects

if – if I can use my sense of humour – God was sort of trying out a physical shape and experimenting and saying, you know, I'll just try out the shape of a man and see how he works as far as breathing and walking and getting on with food. Now that is a possibility, that there were highly developed animals that have all the physical appearance of being human but who are not actually in the image of God, therefore not *biblical* men. Now that is a real possibility. The only thing that worries me about it is that, for example, Neanderthal Man did have funeral rites, which does indicate *some* kind of spiritual perception. But for the rest the scientists have not discovered anything in prehistoric man that indicates he is what we call biblical man in the image of God. They have discovered creatures that have our shape and our size and our style of walking and our jaws but it could be that they were *not* sons of Adam. Now, you can get terribly involved in *this* one. For example, you can say that in Genesis 6 where the sons of God saw the daughters of men, that in fact it was true biblical man falling in love with these other creatures and producing a hybrid giant. It is one possible interpretation of Genesis 6, but I do not think it is the real one. You could also say that these were the creatures that Cain was afraid of being killed by, but I think this is speculation. Number 3, is a possible option.

The fourth theory is held by most Roman Catholic scholars and that is that at some stage in the evolutionary process God changed these highly developed creatures into spiritual beings and that there was a kind of spiritual mutation which God caused which changed prehistoric man into biblical man. Now that is a possibility, but it does not quite seem to fit in with the language of the Bible that I have already outlined; but it is an option which many Christians have adopted.

The fifth possibility is that in fact all the prehistoric men *were* sons of Adam. The problem with that, of course, is that it puts Adam much earlier than we thought he was. It puts him several million years ago at least. And, to say the least, you have problems between Genesis 3, 4 and 5 on that basis.

It must be terribly condensed if Genesis 3 and 4 are meant to cover several million years.

One ingenious speculation is that Adam was not the first man. It is really saying that somebody else was the first man. Perhaps that chap was mentioned even earlier than Adam, Chap 1, have you noticed? But it means that Adam was not Chap 1. Now this may sound a crazy notion but just let me explain it in order to be fair to the Christians who hold it. They notice that in Genesis 1 man is a hunter whereas in Genesis 2 man is a farmer and that the name Adam is not used until Genesis 2. And this theory is that Genesis 1 refers to prehistoric men who *were* in the image of God and that Adam was not the first man but was created later and was more Neolithic Man, agricultural man. And certainly Genesis 2 perfectly fits the Neolithic age from what we know of man's achievements in that age.

Now look, I have given you the five possibilities. I am not going to tell you which one of those I am most inclined to at the moment because the simple fact is that I do not think we have got nearly enough data from the science side to begin to deal with this honestly. They have got a long way to go to make up their minds whether they are really dealing with man or non-man. And until they are much clearer, I do not see the need to let them set my agenda for my thinking. I would only say that I do not believe *anything* has been discovered yet and *proved* by science that prevents my believing that man is a special creation. There are problems but they cannot be resolved until we have more knowledge but there is nothing yet proved that forces me to commit intellectual suicide in believing that God made man a special creation in a way that he did not make... For wherever you place Adam in the family tree, however far away or long ago the first man was created, there is still nothing that has been discovered that ties him in to that process of plants and animals; nothing has yet been proved. So, I am content to wait on this

Chapter 5: Evolution and its effects

one and I hope you are too.

Which raises the question – Why then if it is such an open question, why if science is *nowhere near proving* the evolution of man, why, then, has it been so eagerly believed? Why do people so tumble over each other to say, "Oh but everybody believes in evolution," as if it is a foregone fact when it is just a theory? What is it that has made the world rush like Gadarene swine down the slope into this theory? And the answer is, they *wanted* to believe it. And it may sound extraordinary to you that anybody should want to claim a monkey as their great-grandfather. Most of us are not helped by digging back in our family tree too far and what we discover. Why then was the world so *anxious to believe* that man was part of this whole thing?

We are looking now, not at evolution as a physical idea but as a philosophical ideal. And the reason why it appealed to men's pride to be told that their ancestors were monkeys – which is quite the opposite of what one would expect. I did hear of one Victorian lady who said, "Well we *may* have come from the monkeys but it's not a thing one would talk about." And it obviously hurt *her* pride but for most people, it in fact, inflated their pride to think that we had come all that way up.

Here is Charles Darwin himself; he says, "Man may be excused for feeling some pride at having risen though not through his own exertions to the very summit of the organic scale." And Julian Huxley in our day said, "We may be proud that we are the dominant species." Now, everybody likes to be flattered and we are flattered if we have risen above our background, aren't we? If we feel we are up here when our grandfathers were down there. And I am afraid it appealed to a lot of people's pride. And then Darwin went on to turn the idea into an ideal when he said this. Immediately after saying that we may be excused for feeling some pride at having *risen* to the very summit of the organic scale "and the fact of man's having risen may give him hope for a still higher destiny in the future." Now have you got it? The

CREATION

point at which the idea of where we came *from* became the ideal of where we might *get to*, Charles Darwin himself crossed. So, he turned this idea of where we have come from and he drew a line, a projected line on the graph which said, if we've come all that way from the jungle, where may we not go? And it bolstered the whole idea of progress.

It gripped one of our English Prime Ministers to the point of him issuing an election manifesto in these terms: "Up and up and up and on and on and on" – and he got the election on that slogan. In other words, we are on to the evolutionary escalator, boys, vote us in and we'll take you up and up and up and on and on and on. What a phrase! But it was an evolutionary philosophical ideal that if we have come all that way, then we can keep on going. It is the contrast between the understanding that man is a *fallen* creature and man is a *rising* creature. That is where the rub comes. Do you want to be told you are a fallen woman or a fallen man, or do you want to be told you are a rising man or a rising woman? And so, it appealed not only to pride but it helped us to feel we were going to go up and up and up and on and on and on. And that really fills you with hope for the future.

In other words, it bolsters your ego if you look down on people rather than up, right? When you look at beings above you, whether at work or anywhere else, you feel, "Oh, I fall short; I've got a long way to go." But when you look at all those below you, you tend to think "I'm somebody," right? And what Darwin did was say to man, take your eye off God and the angels and look at the animals. If you think of the angels, you will realise you are down here. If you think of the animals, you will think you are up here. And that appealed quite widely.

But now I come to two very serious matters. First of all, how did this affect people's faith in God? And second, how did it affect their love for men? Here are two key tests. How was their faith in God affected? How was their love for man affected? Because if an idea is right and true, then it ought to help both

Chapter 5: Evolution and its effects

those two things. Faith, hope and love; if you inject a true hope into people, it will increase their faith, increase their love. But if you inject a false hope in, it will destroy faith and destroy love. And the idea of evolution destroyed both faith in God and love for man – and still does. It gives men an excuse not to do either. It is therefore a false hope.

Now, it is interesting that Professor Sedgwick of Cambridge, who was a close friend of Charles Darwin but also a deep, lovely Christian, read *On the Origin of Species* and this was his comment: "It is a dish of rank materialism cleverly cooked and served up merely to make us independent of a Creator." And he was Charles Darwin's best friend but he knew Charles Darwin and he knew that he was a young man running away from God. And he predicted that if his book were believed, the next century would *brutalise* man – that is the word he used. He foresaw wars resulting from Darwin's book on a terrible scale. Now that man, Sedgwick, spotted what was really wrong. Bishop Wilberforce did not; he never tackled it at its real level. He just made a fool of himself and let the church down very badly. But Professor Sedgwick who was, in fact, a *geological* professor interestingly enough realised that what Darwin was really preaching was a materialistic view of life that did not need a Creator. That was where the damage was going to come in.

You see, up until that moment, the greatest argument for God, the strongest argument for God, was the *design* that you could see in nature and suddenly Charles Darwin says, there is no design. It is simply random. Now, do you know the one thing that troubled Charles Darwin until his dying day was his own eye. It was so perfectly designed for the job that he could not bring himself to believe it was random. Because the human eye is so complex, with *millions* of photo cells, that the statistical chances of all the variation changes that were needed producing a human eye were so great that Darwin could never fit it into his theory and he kept being worried about his eyes. They were

CREATION

so perfectly designed. And you see, he was saying there is *no* design, it all happened by accident.

There were other things that he could not cope with; the design of earthworms he found very difficult to cope with. There was too much design in it. Up until then, everybody had said, "You don't believe in God, but look at the design in nature." And Charles Darwin said that there is no design and it troubled him whenever he found it. He just could not come to terms with it. But worse than that, Darwin's view of nature destroyed a view of a good God because *he* saw nature as a struggle for existence – that was his phrase, "struggle for existence". And he saw all these varied species fighting each other to survive and he laid the foundation for that nature red in tooth and claw image we have lived with ever since. And, of course, people could ask how a loving God could create such a mess with species struggling for survival with each other, nature one big warfare?

But there was more than that. He tried desperately to hang on to some belief in God but he failed. At the end of the book *On the Origin of Species* – I have got it on my shelves somewhere – is this sentence: "I see no good reason why the views given in this volume should shock the religious feelings of anyone. There is grandeur in this view of life with its several powers having been originally breathed by the Creator into a few forms or even one." Now, that sounds good; it sounds as if he is a religious man. But I want you to notice first he talks about God as the Creator. He never used any other term for God, and it is interesting that he never called him the Lord, never called him Father, he always simply referred to "the Creator".

Next, I want you to notice that he put God's work at the very beginning and then he was out of the picture. He says, I don't mind God breathing life into the first form but from then on it happened on its own. And in fact, he effectively ruled God out of his own creative activity and virtually said, he may have started it off, but he didn't have anything to do with it thereafter. Now,

Chapter 5: Evolution and its effects

there are many people who believe in a God like that today. They believe God created the world but they do not believe he is still managing it. They do not believe in miracles because they do not believe he is still around. It is called deism. And it is a very common belief that there is a God who wound it all up and set it going but he really does not have anything to do with it now. The weather has nothing to do with God at this moment. He is out of the picture.

And the upshot of it was of course that Darwin's best friends were atheists. Whereas bishops attacked him, atheists like Thomas Huxley flattered him and said, "You've got it boy; we're right with you." It became an embarrassment, in a sense, to him that it was all the *atheists* who flocked to support him and now I am going to tell you the inside story of Charles Darwin, or such bits of it as we need to know. His whole life, his whole *adult* life, was an escape from two people – his earthly father – and his heavenly Father. And he was on the run from both. And it is very interesting to see how our relationships with our earthly father so often colour our relationships with our heavenly Father – and Darwin is no exception. Here is the story.

Darwin was brought up in a good Christian home and Darwin, *as a child*, loved to read his Bible and to pray. Indeed, he would pray; when he had to run a race at school; he would ask the Lord to help him to win. And when he won, he would give a testimony to his schoolmates, that was the Lord who helped me. And he was a devout boy, but as he grew older something began to spoil him and it was that he knew that his father was fabulously wealthy and he lived for the day when his father would die and he would get the money. And that, more than anything else, began to spoil Charles Darwin. And the result was that he was not motivated to study or to work and he became a very deep disappointment to his father. His father tried three careers for him.

First of all, his father sent him up to Edinburgh to train as a medical doctor, of which he was perfectly capable, and when he went there, he went to church and he kept up the religious side. But he didn't study and he didn't work and he told his friends, "It's alright; money's coming to me." And so he was a failure and his father had to bring him home again. And his father said, "Look, you've got to get *some* career; you've got to make your mark." And his father was pushing him all that time. Now this is very interesting. Pushing him into a career but the lad was resisting doing anything serious with his life. He wanted to be a playboy so his father said, what about the ministry? And Charles Darwin thought it might be a good idea and he went off to Cambridge to study theology preparatory to being ordained as a priest in the Church of England. But at Cambridge he got into bad company and he played around and he didn't study and he didn't apply himself. And bit by bit he began to feel more and more guilty about training for the ministry.

He managed to scrape through his degree – just – but he could not face going into the ministry because he was honest enough to admit that he'd had no call from the Lord. Furthermore, by this time he was deeply in debt and he thought, I have disappointed my father twice. He certainly won't pay my debts for me. In fact, when he found out he did. But he said, I just want to go away and do something really interesting and he had been getting interested in biology and so he applied for the job of naturalist on board HMS Beagle and he got the job. It was his way of getting out of the whole situation, getting away from his earthly father and also getting away from his heavenly Father. And from then on, you can trace the decline of his faith until ultimately by the time he was 40 years of age, he said, I'm an agnostic; I do not know if there is a God or not.

It is a tragic story. He kept saying, alright I'll go into the ministry when this voyage is over; I'll go into the ministry when I finish writing up my biology; He kept putting it off. I am glad he never got into the ministry because I do not think he had got a call from God. But he got into this awful tension of

Chapter 5: Evolution and its effects

wanting to believe in God and not wanting to, almost as if God was like his earthly father, and he was wanting to make it and yet not wanting to do what his father told him. And this conflict actually wrecked his health and for most of the rest of his life he was a chronic invalid suffering from headaches, dizziness, vomiting. And yet he was a fit man basically and he lived to an old age but he was a chronic invalid. And any psychologist who examines his diaries and letters will tell you what the problem was. As well as all the physical symptoms, the language of his letters shows that he was suffering from real guilt, that he had never come to terms with the religious side of life. And so, he began to demand more and more proof for faith and first he says in his letters, I no longer believe in the *Old* Testament. A few years later he is saying, I find it difficult to believe the miracles of the *New* Testament and finally he was saying, I find it difficult to believe that the Bible is a divine revelation at all. And a year or two later he says, I'm an agnostic.

Do you know what happened to him as a result? Not only did his health crack but for the rest of his life there was that nervous tension in his mind and the result was the world went dead on him. He lost his love of nature. Once he had marvelled at the beauties he saw on the travels on the Beagle. Now he saw no wonder in it at all. He lost his love of poetry. He lost his love of art. He lost his love of music. This is very interesting. This is what happens to a man who is divided and who is struggling with God and wanting to get away from him. And his interests went down and down and down. Even in his own home he was in conflict because his wife was a lovely Christian and she taught Bible stories to the children and she took them to church and she had them christened and confirmed and she tried but somehow it created an atmosphere in the home in which his wife, he admits, suffered terrible pain because of his attitude. And here is a man who seems to be running away all his life from his background, running away from God. And it was his close friends at Cambridge who spotted the truth. He said that it took him 20 years to arrive at the idea of natural selection through his studies around the world but his friend Sedgwick said, "It didn't take you 20 years. You thought that one up when you were a student; you told it to me. And you said, 'If that was true, then God was not needed.'"

Now, it is fascinating that his friend saw what he was doing. He was trying to find an explanation of the universe that would give him a reason for getting away from the religious side of his life. And that is the inside story. There was no deathbed conversion. That is a Christian rumour. He never repented. What is true is that when he lay dying in Down House and he never went overseas again after the Beagle voyage – the Duke of Argyle came to him and the Duke of Argyle said this to Darwin. He said, "Reading all that you have said about the earthworm" – that was one thing; I forget the other things; he mentioned about three studies that he had done. The Duke of Argyle said, "Doesn't it make you realise what a wonderful Designer our God is?" He said that to Darwin on his deathbed. And the Duke of Argyle recorded later, "I'll never forget Darwin's answer. He said, 'Sometimes that's how it seems to me and other times that just goes away.'" And that is how he died – no faith, no interest in life. Even the beauty of nature left him totally untouched and that is how he ended his days.

And ever since, those who have wanted to escape from God have seized on Darwin's ideas. Those who want to believe that God is not necessary now, that nature can operate itself, that we do not need a Creator, we've got creation, they have seized on this idea, as if they have a fellow feeling with him. The Empress of Prussia read his book – and she was a very good practising Christian – but it destroyed her faith. And you can trace the influence of that woman's life on events in central Europe. I have yet to meet the person who reads any of Darwin's writings and says, "That has really strengthened my faith in God." It never has,

Chapter 5: Evolution and its effects

even though he says at the end it should. Actually, that sentence was put in a later edition as a sop to those who said he was anti-religious. He was not when he wrote it but the seeds of unbelief were already sown in his heart. It is a classic case of where we need to know where a man was going, where he came from and what he was really fighting when he went on that voyage on The Beagle. And who he was running away from.

Now moving from that, which is a sad personal story, I move on to the more serious thing of what happened as his ideas spread, and boy, did they spread! His books were translated into languages all over the world. Suddenly Darwin was being read, but the country where he was read most was a country in the middle of Europe called Germany. But let us just trace it. Professor Sedgwick had said that if Darwin's views were accepted humanity would suffer a damage that would *brutalise* it and sink the human race into a lower grade of degradation than any into which it has fallen since its written records tell us of its history. Now, why did Sedgwick say that? Because there was one idea at the heart of Darwin's teaching which was to do the damage. And the idea was this – to quote Darwin – "From the war of nature, famine and death, the production of *higher* animals directly follows." Can I repeat that? That is one of the most damaging sentences that man has ever written: "From the *war* of nature, famine and death, the production of *higher* animals directly follows." And that idea was *seized* by those who said the way for higher human beings to emerge is war and Adolf Hitler believed Darwin implicitly. He said the only way for the Germans to become the superior race is to wage war, to fight.

Now, that is a pretty alarming thing. Interestingly enough, at first it was not applied to military matters. It was applied in business in America and the businessmen of America read Darwin. Take a man like Andrew Carnegie. I have been to the little poor cottage in Scotland where he first lived. But he went to America and became fabulously wealthy. In his early days in business, he was worried about what he was doing because it seemed against his Christian background but when he read Darwin he said, "It's alright! Business is a struggle for existence and the survival of the fittest." And from then on, he became highly competitive and he used unscrupulous methods. So did many another businessmen in America. They hailed Darwin's teaching and applied it to business and said, "It's cut-throat, it's a jungle and the fittest will survive, [meaning the strongest will survive] and we've just got to fight and get up to the top." And they did not care how they got there, some of them.

John D. Rockefeller did the same thing. When asked to speak in a Sunday School this is how he began: "The growth of large business is merely the survival of the fittest, not an evil tendency but a law of nature and a law of God." And that is what John D. Rockefeller taught Sunday Schools. And you ask, where did he get that from in the Bible? But you know perfectly well where he got it from. He got it from Darwin. But unfortunately, the worst case came in Germany where German thinking was almost universally Darwinian, so much so that the Austrian parliament debated Darwin in parliament and said that it was the most important question that they had to answer, whether Darwin is right or not. And they decided he was right.

There was a philosopher in Germany called Nietzsche and Nietzsche was the thinker behind Adolf Hitler and Nietzsche said, "Darwin has not gone far enough. There is no call to battle to prepare the earth for superman." And then this is what Nietzsche said. I want you to listen carefully to this because this is the issue. He said, "Christianity is the exact reverse of the principle of natural selection. If the degenerate and the sick man is to be of the same value as the healthy man the natural course of evolution is thwarted and the unnatural becomes law." I wonder if you have heard that. Nietzsche said, Christianity looks after the weak; evolution says the strong will survive. And from that teaching came the destruction of the insane in Germany in the

Chapter 5: Evolution and its effects

asylums, of the Gypsies, of the Jews and of anyone who was considered not fit to be part of the superhuman race.

Now it is interesting that all these men picked up the word *struggle* from Darwin – struggle – as if life is a struggle in which the fittest survive by fighting to the top and crushing those beneath them. And if you are not fit to survive it is better that you die. And that word *struggle* in German is *kampf* and when Hitler wrote his book – he only wrote one – he called it *Mein Kampf, My Struggle*. And that whole book is based on Darwin. He is saying that Germans are the superior species and we must crush everybody else. And he got away with it because Germany was reading Darwin and not the Bible. It is frightening to see how far that went in Germany. I know you are probably too young to have experienced the Second World War but I can remember when those camps were opened at the end of the war and the world staggered away in horror thinking, *how* could man in the 20th Century do this? But it was Darwin's teaching that the fittest survive and come to the top of the heap because they are better than the others.

You see, we are not playing around with just a physical idea. This is a philosophical ideal which has *gripped* our world. Now, fascism is how the *right*-wing gripped it but communism is how the *left*-wing gripped it. And Karl Marx wanted to dedicate his book *Das Capital* to Charles Darwin to whom he owed the basic concept of the struggle between the proletariat and the bourgeoisie, the struggle for existence in which the fittest would survive. And the fittest would not be the capitalist but the communist. And so, in Russia today there were compulsory lectures on Darwin, not only to all school children, not only to all students, but even to all prisoners of war. Because that theory of natural selection gave Karl Marx what he called his scientific basis for communism. He writes, "Darwin's book is very important and serves me as a basis in natural science for the struggle in history." And on all communist bookstores you will see Marx, Herbert Spencer, Lenin and Charles Darwin being sold side by side.

So, whether it goes in a right-wing direction into fascism or a left-wing direction into communism, Darwin's ideas have captured our world and I am afraid we only see too late where it all leads and do not realise where it comes from. *And still we dare to feed this ideal into our schools.* It is one of the main reasons why Christians are concerned about state education, that this basic concept is being sown in the minds of the children almost universally in our land. That is where you picked it up and you picked it up from such programmes as David Attenborough's *Life on Earth*. It is being fed to this population consistently and continually. It is a matter for great prayer among Christians. This is one of the reasons I am adding this chapter to give you some feel of the real situation.

Mussolini was dominated by Darwin's view of evolution, just dominated. I could give you all sorts of quotes from Hitler's speeches at Nuremburg. He *hated* the film *Snow White and the Seven Dwarfs*. He forbade it in Germany. Do you know why? Because (in his view) dwarfs have no right to live. They are not fit human beings. He could not cope with any physical imperfection. He wanted a superior race. He wanted the Arian fair-haired boys to breed a super race that would survive by war. This is basically why Russia is prepared to do the same thing. We are living with this. We are living with a quarter of the world that has now swallowed this idea and we must not fool around with that or be under any illusions.

Darwin himself approved of colonisation of Africa because he thought that Europeans were superior to Africans. Did you know that in the Congo when that was colonised, more Africans were slaughtered than died in World War I, I mean than *all* the people that died. And yet it was approved; it was regarded as survival. I heard things said in South Africa such as that the black Africans would take so long to evolve that you couldn't possibly give

Chapter 5: Evolution and its effects

them responsibility. It is amazing how this idea sank into human society that there are superior races and inferior races and that life is a war and a struggle and therefore from this whole thing came the concept that war is good for a nation. I have got quotes here from evolutionists who said that nations need war to make themselves strong to survive. Some of the comments made about the Falkland crisis on TV were of a very similar kind. "It's made us great again"; "It's made us top dog again"; "We needed that war to be *British* again." It is good Darwinianism and we need to label it for what it is.

So, I come to the conclusion now. What is the choice facing us? Well, first it is a *mental* choice but second it is a *moral* choice. Let us look first at the mental choice and just see what the alternative really is. I hardly need to speak here. You can just look at these things and you can see the alternative. The alternative is between a universe that was produced by impersonal chance or by personal choice, a universe that has design in it or disorder in it, a universe that actually was intended or a universe that was an accident, a universe that is an open system in which God can perform miracles or a closed system which operates purely on the so-called "laws of nature". A universe in which either we talk of Father God or Mother Nature, and in the place of the Creator the evolutionist usually talks about nature with a capital N; have you ever noticed that? Nature, capital N, produced this; Nature does that. And most evolutionists I have read actually use the phrase *Mother Nature* as if nature is a person who has now replaced God the Father. That is called in the Bible idolatry, worshipping the creature rather than the Creator. But you see, scientists do not like to talk about Father God now. You embarrass a scientist if you mention God. But talk about Mother Nature and he is not embarrassed in the slightest. Have you ever noticed that?

Teachers will talk to children in school about Mother Nature but are terribly embarrassed to talk about *Father God*. That is the choice. And in the one, the concept of man is that God has made man in *his* image but in the other you are free to make any old god you like in your image, so it looks like freedom on the wrong side. It is not just a mental choice as to what kind of a universe we believe in. Ultimately, the choice you make has moral implications because if you believe in creation, then God is Lord and you are *under divine authority*. Life is a matter of obedience and dependence on him, of remaining childlike and "except you become as little children you don't see the kingdom of God." But on the other side, look what it offers. It offers man as lord. It offers human autonomy; you can do what you like. It offers a life of indulgence not obedience; you can be your own boss and you can fight and the fittest will survive. And you will live in a world of war. That is what it offers. The one is a concept of man falling; the other is a concept of man rising.

Can you see now why people wanted to make that mental choice? That is the choice that Charles Darwin wanted to make. He wanted to go somewhere his father could not tell him what to do. That is the choice he made and he wanted to go somewhere where his heavenly Father could not tell him what to do either. But the ultimate choice you make, I believe, is heaven and hell. Right down the line that is where they both lead. And I do not expect to see Charles Darwin in heaven even though he did pray as a boy. He destroyed his own faith, just destroyed it. So that is the choice that the world is making and that is why it is not just presenting people with facts and letting them choose. I am afraid we are up against the human heart that wants to believe the right-hand side so it is going to be a battle, a real battle. Without the Holy Spirit, you just cannot win it. It takes the Spirit of God to show a man the truth as to why he is really choosing one and not the other. And it is a law of human nature.

It is called Brunner's Law because a man called Brunner first outlined the law. And the law is this. That the more a decision will affect your way of life the more your sinful nature enters into the debate. You see, it is not just a debate as to whether 2 plus 2

Chapter 5: Evolution and its effects

equals 4 or 2 plus 2 equals 5; that is just a mental decision. It does not affect my life tomorrow very deeply. But the evolutionary one *really does*. It creates a whole different world for me to live in, whether I accept creation or evolution basically. And so, I am afraid we are right up against it, the fallen human nature. As Paul says in Romans 1, which is the lesson I quoted earlier, men will hold down the truth in unrighteousness. They actually will choose to believe lies because if they believed the truth they would have to change and so when men do that, what does God do? It says when men give God up, God gives men up to what they want to do. And I am afraid that is what happened to Charles Darwin. He decided to give God up so God gave him up and he lost his interest in music, art, poetry, beauty, nature and he went dead – and that is hell.

Well, that is the choice and it is not just a matter of listening to (or reading) some talks, which I hope have been interesting. It is a whole way of life. There is a creation way of living and there is an evolution way of living. And Karl Marx and Adolf Hitler advocated the evolution way of thinking and the way of living and you can see where it has led. It has led to the slaughter of *millions* of *innocent* people but that is the theory. That is how life is supposed to be under that theory and I just praise God that he is the kind of God who did not make a world in which men would survive because they were strong and fit but that when Jesus came, he came to preach the gospel to the poor, to bring liberty to the captive, to get the lame walking again. And the people whom nobody else valued he befriended. They criticised him for it. But he was showing what God is like and it is a totally different world to the world of Charles Darwin.

BOOKS BY DAVID PAWSON
AVAILABLE FROM DAVIDPAWSON.COM

BIBLE COMMENTARIES

UNLOCKING THE BIBLE Omnibus ISBN 978 0 007166 66 4
UNLOCKING THE BIBLE - Charts, diagrams and images ISBN 978 1 911173 17 5

Introducing GENESIS ISBN 978 1 911173 80 9
Introducing The OLD TESTAMENT and HEBREW POETRY ISBN 978 1 911173 90 8

A Commentary on GENESIS Chapters 1-25 ISBN 978 1 911173 82 3
A Commentary on EXODUS ISBN 978 1 911173 85 4
A Commentary on Selected PSALMS ISBN 978 1 911173 91 5
A Commentary on ECCLESIASTES ISBN 978 1 911173 98 4
A Commentary on ISAIAH ISBN 978 1 913472 05 4
A Commentary on JEREMIAH ISBN 978 1 911173 76 2
A commentary on DANIEL ISBN 978 1 911173 06 9
A Commentary on THE MINOR PROPHETS ISBN 978 1 911173 94 6
A Commentary on ZECHARIAH ISBN 978 1 911173 38 0

A Commentary on the Gospel of MATTHEW ISBN 978 1 913472 09 2
A Commentary on the Gospel of MARK ISBN 978 1 909886 26 1
A Commentary on the Gospel of LUKE ISBN 978 1 911173 21 2
A Commentary on the Gospel of JOHN ISBN 978 1 909886 27 8
A Commentary on ACTS ISBN 978 1 909886 38 4
A Commentary on ROMANS ISBN 978 1 909886 78 0
A Commentary on 1 & 2 CORINTHIANS ISBN 978 1 909886 95 7
A Commentary on GALATIANS ISBN 978 1 909886 29 2
A Commentary on EPHESIANS ISBN 978 1 909886 98 8
A Commentary on PHILIPPIANS ISBN 978 1 909886 74 2
A Commentary on COLOSSIANS ISBN 978 1 913472 17 7
A Commentary on 1 & 2 THESSALONIANS ISBN 978 1 909886 73 5
A Commentary on 1 & 2 TIMOTHY, TITUS, PHILEMON - The Personal Letters ISBN 978 1 909886 70 4
A Commentary on HEBREWS ISBN 978 1 909886 33 9
A Commentary on JAMES ISBN 978 1 909886 72 8
A commentary on 1 & 2 PETER ISBN 978 1 909886 79 7
A Commentary on the LETTERS OF JOHN ISBN 978 1 909886 69 8
A Commentary on JUDE ISBN 978 1 909886 28 5
A Commentary on the book of REVELATION ISBN 978 1 909886 25 4

EXPLAINING SERIES
A CHRISTIAN DISCIPLESHIP PROGRAMME

THE AMAZING STORY OF JESUS ISBN 978 1 911173 29 8
THE RESURRECTION: The Heart of Christianity ISBN 978 1 911173 30 4
STUDYING THE BIBLE ISBN 978 1 911173 31 1
NEW TESTAMENT BAPTISM ISBN 978 1 911173 33 5
BEING ANOINTED AND FILLED WITH THE HOLY SPIRIT ISBN 978 1 911173 18 2
ETERNALLY SECURE? What the Bible says about being saved ISBN 978 1 911173 19 9
GRACE AND SALVATION: Generous, Undeserved, Co-Operation ISBN 978 1 911173 99 1
THE KEY STEPS TO BECOMING A CHRISTIAN ISBN 978 1 911173 87 8
THE TRINITY ISBN 978 1 911173 07 6
HOW TO STUDY A BOOK OF THE BIBLE: JUDE ISBN 978 1 911173 34 2
THE TRUTH ABOUT CHRISTMAS ISBN 978 1 911173 77 9
END TIMES ISBN 978 1 911173 46 5
WHAT THE BIBLE SAYS ABOUT WORK ISBN 978 1 911173 36 6
WHAT THE BIBLE SAYS ABOUT MONEY ISBN 978 1 911173 35 9
GRACE: Undeserved Favour, Irresistible Force or Unconditional Forgiveness?
ISBN 978 1 909886 84 1
THREE TEXTS OFTEN TAKEN OUT OF CONTEXT: Expounding the truth and exposing error
ISBN 978 1 909886 85 8
BUILDING A NEW TESTAMENT CHURCH ISBN 978 1 911173 69 4
DE-GREECING THE CHURCH: The impact of Greek thinking on Christian beliefs
ISBN 978 1 911173 20 5

TOPICAL BOOKS

Angels ISBN 978 1 909886 02 5
A Preacher's Legacy ISBN 978 1 911173 27 4
By God, I Will - The Biblical Covenants ISBN 978 1 909886 21 6
Christianity Explained ISBN 978 1 909886 64 3
Completing Luther's Reformation ISBN 978 1 911173 26 7
Defending Christian Zionism ISBN 978 1 909886 31 5
Heaven and Hell: A message of hope and warning to believers ISBN 978 1 913472 25 2
Is John 3:16 the Gospel? ISBN 978 1 909886 62 9
Israel in the New Testament (includes Galatians) ISBN 978 1 909886 57 5
Jesus Baptises In One Holy Spirit ISBN 978 1 909886 66 7
JESUS: The Seven Wonders of HIStory ISBN 978 1 909886 24 7
Kingdoms in Conflict ISBN 978 1 909886 04 9
Leadership Is Male ISBN 978 1 909886 67 4
Living in Hope ISBN 978 1 909886 65 0
Loose Leaves from My Bible ISBN 978 1 909886 55 1
Men for God ISBN 978 1 913472 20 7
Not As Bad As The Truth (David's Autobiography) ISBN 978 1 913472 35 1
Once Saved, Always Saved? ISBN 978 1 913472 27 6
Practising the Principles of Prayer ISBN 978 1 909886 63 6
Remarriage is Adultery Unless ... ISBN 978 1 909886 22 3
Simon Peter: The Reed and the Rock ISBN 978 1 909886 23 0
The Character of God ISBN 978 1 909886 34 6
The Challenge of Islam to Christians ISBN 978 1 913472 34 4
The God and the Gospel of Righteousness ISBN 978 1 909886 68 1
The Lord's Prayer ISBN 978 1 909886 71 1
The Maker's Instructions - A new look at the 10 Commandments
ISBN 978 1 909886 30 8
The Normal Christian Birth ISBN 978 1 913472 36 8
The Road To Hell ISBN 978 1 909886 59 9
Tributes by Friends of David Pawson ISBN 978 1 913472 21 4
Understanding the Resurrection ISBN 978 1 911173 22 9
Understanding the Second Coming ISBN 978 1 911173 23 6
Understanding Water Baptism ISBN 978 1 911173 24 3
What the Bible says about the Holy Spirit ISBN 978 1 909886 54 4
What I'm Looking Forward To: Life After Life After Death ISBN 978 1 913472 26 9
When Jesus Returns ISBN 978 1 913472 33 7
Where has the Body been for 2000 years? - Church history for beginners
ISBN 978 1 909886 20 9
Where is Jesus Now? ISBN 978 1 911173 78 6
Why Does God Allow Natural Disasters? ISBN 978 1 909886 58 2
Word And Spirit Together ISBN 978 1 909886 60 5

www.ingramcontent.com/pod-product-compliance
Lightning Source LLC
Chambersburg PA
CBHW050412120526
44590CB00015B/1941